A cheetah cub nuzzles its mother as she keeps watch for predators.

A lion yawns in the midday heat, in Zakouma National Park, in Chad, Africa.

THE ULTIMATE BOOK OF BIG CATS

YOUR GUIDE TO THE SECRET LIVES OF THESE FIERCE, FABULOUS FELINES

STEVE WINTER AND **SHARON GUYNUP**

NATIONAL GEOGRAPHIC
Washington, D.C.

CONTENTS

Snow leopard

Lion

INTRODUCTION

A young male tiger walks through tall elephant grass in Kaziranga National Park, in India, and takes his own picture in a camera trap.

Meet Steve

COMING FACE-TO-FACE WITH BIG CATS IS THRILLING, MAGICAL, SOMETIMES SCARY—AND UTTERLY UNFORGETTABLE.

From Asia to South America, I met wild jaguars, tigers, lions, cheetahs, leopards, cougars, and some smaller cats. But my first encounters are deeply etched in my memories.

I spent months slogging through rainforests trying to photograph jaguars, but I only glimpsed tracks. Sometimes those tracks were in my own footprints: A cat was following me! Finally, in Brazil, I learned that a huge male jaguar was often seen on a nearby ranch around sunset. A jaguar expert drove me there. Through binoculars, I spotted the cat in the distance. I got out of the truck and followed it for about 20 minutes as it walked on a dirt road—and then it disappeared, almost like a ghost.

I whispered to my guide, "Where did it go?" Then suddenly, I saw the jaguar staring at me from the grass just ahead. I froze. My heart was pounding, and my hands shook as I raised the camera and took pictures. My guide warned me that the cat's ears were flat on its head, meaning that it was agitated and could pounce. We backed away slowly. The cat sauntered off. That did it: I was forever captivated by big cats.

I WAS IN THE JUNGLE IN INDIA WHEN I GLIMPSED MY FIRST WILD CAT.

A Bengal tiger emerged from the forest, walking toward my Jeep. I was awestruck by its gorgeous markings—and surprised that it looked so slim. Then the cat turned, and I saw its huge girth and incredibly long body. It was stunning, rippling with muscles and glowing orange in the sunlight. In that moment, I understood why people have feared and revered tigers throughout history.

Steve and I have been awed by the power and beauty of the world's wild cats for the more than 20 years we've studied, photographed, filmed, and written about them. We want to share what we've learned about their mysterious lives, secret behaviors, and amazing anatomy; their superpower leaping, racing, and hunting abilities; how and where they raise their cubs; their prehistoric ancestors; and how they've been worshipped as gods across the world.

We also try to give these animals a voice. Big cats may rule the landscapes they live in, but all are threatened. Some are critically endangered.

We hope that in learning about wild cats, you'll be as fascinated by them as we are—and understand how important these awesome animals are to maintaining a healthy planet.

Meet Sharon

CHAPTER ONE

THE **SUPER** SEVEN

Jaguar

>>> VERY FEW ANIMALS ARE BOTH ADORABLE AND DEADLY, PLAYFUL AND POWERFUL, AND CHILLED OUT AND COMPETITIVE. But these cool cats sure are!

Of the 41 species of wild cats on the planet, only seven of them are the mighty big cats. Four of these can roar: tigers, lions, leopards, and jaguars. The other three big cats—snow leopards, cougars, and cheetahs—can't roar, but they can purr! The size of these cats—up to 575 pounds (261 kg)—isn't their only extraordinary trait. They're strong: Jaguars have the most powerful jaws of any mammal. They're swift: Cheetahs are the world's fastest land animals. They're graceful: Leopards climb effortlessly up trees, and snow leopards and cougars leap with exceptional ease. They're powerful: Lions can take down prey several times their size. They're intriguing: These cats have been revered—and even worshipped—for thousands of years. They're familiar: They may be huge, but big cats look—and sometimes even behave!—like our own pet kitties.

Get ready to sink your teeth into the worlds of these seven spectacular cats—and their smaller cousins—to find out the many ways these cats are alike and what makes some of them utterly unique.

ONE BIG CAT FAMILY

>>> **ALL CATS—FROM THE DOMESTIC CAT THAT SNOOZES ON YOUR COUCH TO LIONS THAT ROAM AFRICA'S GRASSY PLAINS—SHARE A COMMON ANCESTOR.** This means that whether they are massive or tiny, tame or wild, every cat is part of the Felidae family.

Paramachairodus

Metailurus

Proailurus

Pseudaelurus

Branching Out

Seven cats in this book are officially called big cats, but they fall on two different branches of the Felidae family tree. Tigers, lions, leopards, jaguars, and snow leopards share one branch. They have their own scientific classification, or genus: *Panthera.* The other two species, cougars and cheetahs, live on a separate branch of the family tree and have different characteristics.

Small- and medium-size cats make up the other 34 species. Unlike their larger cousins, they aren't usually the top predators in their habitats. But they are fierce, strong, and agile in their own right. (Stay tuned—you'll find out about many of them on pages 66-69.)

It Runs in the Family

All cats have super senses: They see, smell, and hear exceptionally well. They are known for their sharp claws, which they use for hunting, climbing, and scratching. Their powerful jaws and sharp teeth are made for biting and tearing because cats are carnivores, or meat-eaters.

Few species can match these cats' strength and grace when running, climbing, or leaping. But each of these magnificent felines has its own special traits and adaptations that allow it to thrive in its environment. So don't go calling them copycats!

36.5–23.5 MILLION YEARS AGO

23.5–5.3 MILLION YEARS AGO

Homotherium

Machairodus

Megantereon

Smilodon

Felis (house cats)

Dinofelis

Puma (cougars)

Acinonyx (cheetahs)

Miracinonyx

Leopardus (small wild cats native to the Americas, like ocelots)

Neofelis (clouded leopards)

Panthera (jaguars, leopards, tigers, lions, and snow leopards)

NEXT-OF-KIN KITTY

How closely is your house cat related to a wild cat?

>>> **HAVE YOU EVER WATCHED YOUR CAT ON THE PROWL ... SAY, FOR A FLY THAT'S LANDED ON A WINDOW?** First, the cat slinks down low, slowly swishing its tail while keeping its eyes trained on its target. Then it springs in a lightning-fast pounce, throwing itself at the window with a thud—and the fly zips away. Even though your kitty isn't exactly the king of the jungle, it has the same hunting instincts as a lion. That's because your pet is a distant relative of every big cat. They all share a common ancestor that emerged in what is now Europe some 10 or 11 million years ago.

Cats likely domesticated themselves thousands of years ago. When nomadic humans first settled in villages and began to grow crops, rodents swarmed in and infested places where grain was stored. Wild cats followed and made themselves useful, getting rid of the pesky rodents. But the first evidence of people actually living with cats was found on the Mediterranean island of Cyprus. Archaeologists unearthed the remains of a human and a cat buried together that dated back more than 11,000 years to 9500 B.C. Around that time, people started keeping the small tabbylike wild cat *Felis silvestris lybica* as a pet.

Today's domestic cats may have come a long way from their wild roots, but they are still surprisingly similar to their big cat cousins.

Male lion

CRAZY FOR
CATNIP

Your kitty isn't the only feline that goes bonkers for catnip. In the 1970s, zoologists gave catnip to 33 big cats at a zoo in Knoxville, Tennessee, U.S.A. The jaguars and lions had the strongest reactions. They rolled around, and sniffed, licked, and rubbed on the catnip for an hour. They were far more responsive than a house cat, which spent just 15 minutes investigating the mintlike plant. The tigers, cougars, and bobcats were even less interested. The cheetahs ignored it altogether.

Siberian tiger

THEY'RE
CHEEKY

When your cat rubs up against you, it's showing affection, right? Wrong! It is actually depositing its scent on you, "marking" just like big cats do. By rubbing, your cat is marking you as part of its territory.

TIGER
CAT

Even if your kitty doesn't have stripes, it's more tiger than you might think. When researchers analyzed the DNA of a Siberian tiger, they discovered that it shares 95.6 percent of its genes with domestic cats. This makes the two cats closer relatives than humans and gorillas, which have a 94.8 percent genetic similarity.

TIGERS

>>> AS THE KINGS AND QUEENS OF ASIA'S JUNGLES, GRASSLANDS, AND DESERTS, TIGERS ARE THE LARGEST OF THE WORLD'S CATS.

They're adaptable, too: They thrive in a range of habitats, from the frigid Himalayan foothills to mangrove swamps. Tigers are the only striped big cat, and each individual has its own pattern that is as unique as a human fingerprint. This allows scientists to identify and track specific tigers.

Tigers reign as the top predator in every ecosystem they inhabit. They're carnivores, or meat-eaters, that feast on everything from deer and wild boar to monkeys and buffalo, depending on where they live. These powerful cats stalk their prey silently, usually in the murky light of morning and evening. They use their massive canine teeth, which are the largest of any land-dwelling carnivore, to kill with a bite to the throat.

Except for females that are caring for their cubs and pairs that come together to mate, these cats live a solitary life. Nine subspecies once roamed through 21 countries, from Siberia's forests southward to Indonesia's tropical jungles, and from present-day Turkey to China. Three of those cats are gone. The last known Bali tiger disappeared during the 1930s. Both the Javan and Caspian tigers went extinct in the 1970s. Six subspecies remain in 11 countries, and one of them, the South China tiger, exists only in captivity. Tigers are the most endangered of all the big cats: Less than 4,000 tigers remain in the wild.

Siberian Tiger

SCIENTIFIC NAME: *Panthera tigris altaica*

WEIGHT: Up to 560 pounds (254 kg)

RANGE: Russian Far East; northeast China

Siberian tigers, also known as Amur tigers, live in thick forests in far eastern Russia; a few remain across the border in China. This subspecies evolved to survive the frigid Siberian winters, with its exceptionally thick, fluffy winter coat and the largest ruff around its neck of all the tigers. In winter, their fur may be shaded a lighter orange for better camouflage in the snow, and some have paler stripes than other tigers. They were last counted in 2015; researchers estimate that between 480 and 540 Siberian tigers remain in the wild.

Bengal Tiger

SCIENTIFIC NAME: *Panthera tigris tigris*

WEIGHT: Up to 716 pounds (325 kg)

RANGE: Myanmar, Bangladesh, India, Nepal, and Bhutan

Most of the world's wild tigers—approximately two-thirds—are Bengals. They're also the biggest tigers, weighing as much as 57 house cats! The tiger is deeply woven into mythology and religion both in Bangladesh and in neighboring India, where it is also the national animal. India is home to most of the world's tigers. The last time they counted them, Indian scientists set up 26,000 camera traps in places where Bengals are known to live. They also deployed thousands of park guards and researchers who walked about 310,000 miles (500,000 km) looking for signs of the cats. They counted 2,967 Bengals.

TIGERS
>> CONTINUED

TO **LURE** ONE OF **THEIR** FAVORITE **PREY, TIGERS IMITATE THE** "**POOK**" **SOUND** THAT SAMBAR DEER MAKE.

Indochinese Tiger

SCIENTIFIC NAME: *Panthera tigris corbetti*

WEIGHT: Up to 430 pounds (195 kg)

RANGE: Thailand and Myanmar

Indochinese tigers are also very rare: Just a few hundred remain. In recent years, they have disappeared from Cambodia, Vietnam, and Laos. Compared with other tigers, this cat's coat is darker with narrow stripes.

Malayan Tiger

SCIENTIFIC NAME: *Panthera tigris jacksoni*

WEIGHT: Up to 265 pounds (120 kg) (estimated)

RANGE: Malay Peninsula; southern tip of Thailand

In 2004, scientists discovered a new tiger! For a long time, Malayan tigers were mistakenly believed to be Indochinese tigers because they're almost the exact same size and weight. But advanced DNA testing methods revealed that they are actually a separate subspecies. They're critically endangered: Only 80 to 100 Malayan tigers are thought to remain. They're confined to just a small region, mostly the tropical rainforests of the Malay Peninsula in Southeast Asia.

Sumatran Tiger

SCIENTIFIC NAME: *Panthera tigris sumatrae*

WEIGHT: Up to 308 pounds (140 kg)

RANGE: Sumatra, Indonesia

With a whitish mane that frames its head, the Sumatran tiger almost looks like a cross between a lion and a tiger. Its rusty orange coat has many thin stripes, which help conceal it in the dense rainforest. It's the smallest tiger. It lives on the isolated island of Sumatra, in Indonesia. This tiger evolved to be just large enough to capture available prey, but not so big that it wouldn't have enough to eat.

South China Tiger

SCIENTIFIC NAME: *Panthera tigris amoyensis*

WEIGHT: Up to 330 pounds (150 kg)

RANGE: Captive tiger facilities; China

It's true: No two tigers share the same stripes. But the South China tiger is quite different from its cousins. Its unique stripes are broad and spaced far apart, which helped it camouflage among the reeds in the wet forests where it once lived in central and southern China. This cat has not been seen in the wild since the early 1970s and is believed to be extinct: It only remains in captivity, mostly in China.

LIONS

>>> **LIONS ARE OFTEN CALLED THE "KING OF THE JUNGLE," BUT THEY DON'T LIVE IN THE JUNGLE.** Their power and majestic presence likely inspired this nickname, but they are not stronger or more courageous than other big cats. They do, however, have very different living arrangements. Lions are the extroverts of the big cat family. While most big cats live and hunt alone, lions are social animals. They live in family groups, called prides, with anywhere from three to 40 members. And unlike their big cat cousins, lions are not elusive. Quite the opposite! Most of the world's lions live right out in the open on the African savanna, so they are relatively easy to spot.

A pride is usually headed by one dominant male. He defends his pride's territory with fearsome roars that can be heard five miles (8 km) away, and he may fight intruders to the death.

Meanwhile, the females do most of the hunting. (Though the males often eat first.) Many of the hoofed animals they pursue are large and fast, but lions work as a team to improve their odds of catching a meal.

AFRICAN LION

SCIENTIFIC NAME: *Panthera leo*

WEIGHT: Up to 575 pounds (261 kg)

RANGE: Sub-Saharan Africa

With teamwork, these fierce, tawny predators can take down bigger prey than their larger cousin, the tiger, can—huge animals like 1,910-pound (866-kg) African buffaloes or 3,000-pound (1,360-kg) giraffes. But African lions also welcome an easy meal, taking over a kill made by wild dogs, leopards, or hyenas. They rest between hunts and may sleep—or just doze—up to 20 hours a day! As cubs, they're known for their cuddly, playful antics.

One researcher discovered that **LIONS CAN COUNT.** They listen and count the roars from another lion pride to determine how many cats are in the group.

ASIATIC LION

SCIENTIFIC NAME: *Panthera leo persica*

WEIGHT: Up to 420 pounds (190 kg)

RANGE: Gujarat, India

Asiatic lions—the African lion's slightly smaller, less social cousin—once lived across Asia, from Turkey throughout the Middle East to India. One small, critically endangered population still survives in India's Gir Forest. These lions live in prides, but males tend to live separately or sometimes in small groups, except when it's time to mate or when they want to share a big kill. The males have skimpy, sparse manes, which make their ears look more prominent. Some even have a bald spot on top of their heads.

SNOW LEOPARDS

>>> PEOPLE WHO LIVE IN THE HIMALAYA IN ASIA SHARE THEIR HOMELAND WITH THE SNOW LEOPARD: AN ANIMAL THAT'S SO ELUSIVE IT'S KNOWN AS THE "GHOST OF THE MOUNTAINS" OR THE "GRAY GHOST." These mysterious cats live at the top of the world in the treeless, rugged mountains of Central Asia at altitudes up to 18,000 feet (5,500 m)—as high as the base camps on Mount Everest!

Snow leopards evolved to survive in this brutally cold, high-altitude climate where winter temperatures dip to minus 58°F (-50°C). Their luxurious coats, with rose-shaped "rosette" spots, insulate them from the harsh weather. With 26,000 hairs per square inch (6 sq cm), it is the thickest coat of any cat's. (Your head only has about 1,300 hairs per square inch [6 sq cm].) Fur on the bottom of their paws keeps them from slipping on snow and ice, and their big paws work like snowshoes to keep them from sinking into deep drifts.

At more than three feet (0.9 m) long, a snow leopard's tail is almost as long as the rest of its body—the longest of any cat's. To stay warm, a snow leopard tucks its nose under its tail and wraps it around itself like a furry scarf. Its tail also provides balance—almost like the rudder on a ship—when its chasing its prey through steep, rocky terrain. Snow leopards hunt whatever is available, from small marmots and wild blue sheep to domesticated goats and yaks. They may roam across an area half the size of Alaska, U.S.A., to find food.

A snow leopard's paw print in the snow

SNOW LEOPARD

SCIENTIFIC NAME: *Panthera uncia*

WEIGHT: Up to 121 pounds (55 kg)

RANGE: Central and South Asia

Snow leopards' fur ranges from silvery gray to pale gold, dotted with dark rosettes (markings that resemble a rose). From afar, their rosettes look like shadows, and their lighter underbelly reflects the color of the ground, allowing them to blend in unseen in their mountain home.

JAGUARS

>>> THE NAME "JAGUAR" MAY HAVE COME FROM THE NATIVE AMERICAN WORD *YAGUARETÉ*, WHICH TRANSLATES TO "A BEAST THAT KILLS ITS PREY WITH A SINGLE BOUND." That's an accurate description for this big cat, which is known to ambush its prey on land and in the water.

Jaguars are also known as *tigre americano*, or the American tiger. They live across the Americas from Mexico to Argentina, and they're the biggest cat in the Western Hemisphere. Every now and then, a jaguar is spotted in the southwestern United States where they used to live. Most live in the Amazon rainforest or in Brazil's Pantanal, a massive wetland area. They vary in size—jaguars in Central America may be about half the size of jaguars in the Pantanal—but there are no jaguar subspecies.

Like most big cats, jaguars live alone, except for females that are raising cubs. They are crepuscular, meaning that they are most active in the dim light of dusk and dawn. Jaguars usually sleep through the heat of the day, nestled under a tree, on top of a rock, or on a shady riverbank.

Jaguars eat almost anything—at least 85 different species! **THEY ARE POWERFUL SWIMMERS AND REGULARLY HUNT** by diving into the water, where they spend more time than any other big cat.

A jaguar lunges after a caiman in a river in Brazil.

JAGUAR

SCIENTIFIC NAME:	*Panthera onca*
WEIGHT:	Up to 348 pounds (158 kg)
RANGE:	South and Central America

The jaguar's stocky, compact, muscular body radiates the power of a prizefighter, and its daggerlike, two-inch (5-cm)-long canines make it even more formidable. Its beautiful coat ranges in color from pale yellow to golden brown and is dotted with black rosette markings similar to a leopard's, but the jaguar's rosettes are larger, with a black dot in the middle. These spots help the cat fade into its surroundings to stage a surprise attack.

COUGARS

>>> COUGARS—ALSO KNOWN AS MOUNTAIN LIONS, PUMAS, PANTHERS, AND BY OTHER NAMES—MIGHT NOT BE THE BIGGEST BIG CAT, BUT THEIR RANGE IS MASSIVE. They live across the North American continent, from northern Canada to swamps in southern Florida, U.S.A., and then all the way down to the tip of South America. They require a lot of room to roam and are at home living among mountain peaks and in thick forests, rocky deserts, tropical jungles, and even suburbs and cities. Yet like the snow leopard, the cougar is also a "ghost cat," rarely seen.

These cats are ambush hunters that eat everything from birds and large rodents to deer and elk. When they successfully hunt a large animal, cougars often drag it to a spot where they can "cache" it. They hide it under leaves, dirt, or a log and continue to eat it for a few days or for up to four weeks in winter.

Unlike the five *Panthera* big cats, cougars don't roar. Instead, they communicate with a lot of un-big-cat-like sounds: They yowl, chirp like a bird, mew and purr like a house cat, and screech in a way that sounds like a person screaming!

COUGAR

SCIENTIFIC NAME: *Puma concolor*

WEIGHT: Up to 176 pounds (80 kg)

RANGE: North America, Central America, and South America

A cougar has a slender body, pointy ears, and light gray, tan, or even brick-red fur. Its cream-colored underbelly and the dark fur behind its ears and on the tip of its tail help it stay hidden when it's stalking its prey.

This cat is a mighty leaper. It's been seen clearing a nine-foot (2.7-m) fence with a sheep in its mouth. And with a running start, a cougar can jump up to 40 feet (12 m) in one forward stride.

FLORIDA PANTHER

SCIENTIFIC NAME: *Puma concolor coryi*

WEIGHT: Up to 160 pounds (73 kg)

RANGE: Florida, U.S.A.

Florida panthers are the only population of cougars living east of the Mississippi River in the United States. About 50 years ago, perhaps 20 were left in the wild, and only about three females were the right age to have cubs. With intensive protection—and the addition of a few cougars brought in from Texas, U.S.A.—they've made a comeback. Though they're still endangered, about 200 prowl southwest Florida today. With so few panthers in the gene pool, some Florida panthers have developed signs of inbreeding: health problems caused by mating with close relatives. Some have heart complications or are unable to have cubs. Others have physical signs of inbreeding: a cow-lick and a kink at the end of their tails.

LEOPARDS

>>> **LEOPARDS ARE EXTREMELY ADAPTABLE CATS.** They are strong, skillful hunters and will eat almost anything that comes close enough to catch. They can thrive just about anywhere, from Middle Eastern deserts and rugged mountains to African rainforests. Some even live on the outskirts of big cities, but most prowl forests or grasslands. In all, nine leopard subspecies live in Africa, Asia, and the Middle East, and all are threatened, endangered, or critically endangered.

Their cream-colored or brownish fur, marked with signature black rosette spots, serves as camouflage in the dappled sun and leafy shade of a tree or helps them blend in with dry savanna grasses.

Compared to other wild cats, the leopard has a long body, relatively short legs, and a big head. While it resembles the jaguar, it is smaller and lighter.

A LEOPARD'S ROSETTES ARE DIFFERENT THAN A JAGUAR'S: There are more of them, they're smaller, and they have brown or gold centers with no spot in the middle. The spots on a leopard's face are solid black.

Leopard

LEOPARD

SCIENTIFIC NAME: *Panthera pardus*

WEIGHT: Up to 198 pounds (90 kg)

RANGE: Sub-Saharan Africa

The most well-known leopard is the African leopard. To spot one, sometimes it's best to look up! Most leopards live in forests or grasslands. But these cats are expert climbers and spend plenty of time perched high in the trees. After a hunt, they often drag their meal up into the branches to eat in a safe place, protected from other carnivore competitors.

CHEETAHS

>>> **THE CHEETAH IS THE OLYMPIC RUNNER OF BIG CATS.**
Its lanky, well-muscled body is built for speed. It is the fastest land animal on Earth! When it is running at top speed, a cheetah's extremely long, thin legs and unusually long spine allow it to cover 21 feet (6.4 m) in a single stride.

A cheetah's hind legs reach almost to its ears before flying back, and during its stride it catches air, with all four paws lifted off the ground. It digs into the ground for extra traction with its blunt claws, kind of like soccer cleats. A cheetah's claws don't retract like those of other big cats.

With an extra large heart and lungs and big nostrils that allow for more oxygen to reach its muscles, a cheetah can sprint at speeds up to 70 miles an hour (113 km/h). And it can accelerate from zero to 45 miles an hour (72 km/h) in just 2.5 seconds. That's fast!

CHEETAH

SCIENTIFIC NAME: *Acinonyx jubatus*

WEIGHT: Up to 141 pounds (64 kg)

RANGE: Parts of Africa

This tall, high-speed hunter inhabits a large part of Africa. Unlike other big cats, cheetahs prefer daytime hunting, using their keen eyesight to their advantage: They can see fine details two miles (3 km) away! Black "tear" streaks on either side of a cheetah's nose reflect the sun's glare, acting much like the eye black that some baseball and football players wear.

ASIATIC CHEETAH

SCIENTIFIC NAME: *Acinonyx jubatus venaticus*

WEIGHT: Up to 119 pounds (54 kg)

RANGE: Iran

The last critically endangered Asiatic cheetahs survive in small, isolated groups in remote corners of Iran. They once ranged across the Middle East all the way to Russia; today perhaps 50 are left in the wild. Asiatic cheetahs have been kept in captivity for more than 4,000 years. They were considered the easiest big cat to tame, and rulers, including Genghis Khan, used them as hunting partners in Asia.

"Over the many years I've spent on assignment in the wild, some of my most amazing experiences have been photographing cubs—like these three cheetahs I encountered in South Africa. I watched their every move as they learned to stalk, pounce, and perfect the skills they need to survive. It gives me hope because they're the next generation!"
—Steve Winter

A BIG CAT WORLD

Big cats are globe-trotters! They're found on most continents in the world except Antarctica, Australia, and Europe. Their homes are as diverse as they are: icy mountains, steamy mangrove swamps, brutally hot savannas and deserts, thick forests, and major metropolitan cities. Check out the map below and see where on Earth the seven big cats live.

NORTH AMERICA

ATLANTIC OCEAN

AFR

SOUTH AMERICA

PACIFIC OCEAN

SOUTHERN OCEAN

Cougar habitat

INCLUDES: forests, deserts, grasslands, savannas, and scrublands

Jaguar habitat

INCLUDES: rainforests, scrublands, wetlands, and savannas

Cougar

Jaguar

ARCTIC OCEAN

EUROPE

ASIA

Snow Leopard habitat

INCLUDES: shrublands, rocky areas, grasslands, and high mountains

Snow leopard

Tiger

Tiger habitat

INCLUDES: tropical rainforests, evergreen forests, temperate forests, mangrove swamps, grasslands, savannas, and mountains

PACIFIC OCEAN

ICA

Leopard habitat

INCLUDES: forests, deserts, rocky areas, grasslands, savannas, mountains, cities, and shrublands

INDIAN OCEAN

AUSTRALIA

Leopard

Lion habitat

INCLUDES: open woodlands, thick grasslands, and dense shrublands

Cheetah habitat

INCLUDES: grasslands, dry forests, savannas, and shrublands

Lion

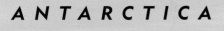
Cheetah

ANTARCTICA

33

WHAT'S IN A NAME?

> **SOME CATS HAVE TOO MANY NAMES TO KEEP TRACK OF.** Indigenous communities have their own names for the cats that live nearby. Early European explorers made up names for animals they encountered. And some big cats got special nicknames.

HELLO, MY NAME IS ... COUGAR?

The cougar holds the world record for the animal species with the most names. It has more than 40 names in the English language alone. Depending on the place, it's known as a mountain lion, panther, catamount, ghost cat, mountain devil, painter, shadow cat, silver lion, or mountain screamer. The Inca named the cat "puma." Early Spanish explorers who came to the Americas called them *león*, Spanish for "lion," and *gato monte*, "cat of the mountain." The name "cougar" came from a native South American word, *cuguacuarana*, that was misspelled and shortened. Its scientific name is *Puma concolor*.

A male panther leaps over a creek in Florida Panther National Wildlife Refuge, in Florida, U.S.A.

BLACK PANTHER: EXPLAINED

Black Panther is a Marvel superhero, but a black panther is not a species of cat: It's either a leopard or a jaguar. These cats have a genetic mutation that increases the amount of black pigment in their skin and fur. Called melanistic, these cats are the opposite of albinos, which are born without any pigment in their skin or fur. Dark fur gives a black panther the perfect cover for nighttime hunting in thick forests. Bobcats, lynx, jaguarundis, and a few other smaller cats can also have black coats. While they appear jet black, they do have spots—it's just hard to see them from far away or in low light.

A male leopard with a melanistic female in India

SIZING UP SUPERSIZE CATS

Exactly how big are big cats? Check out how they compare in weight to other animals and everyday items.

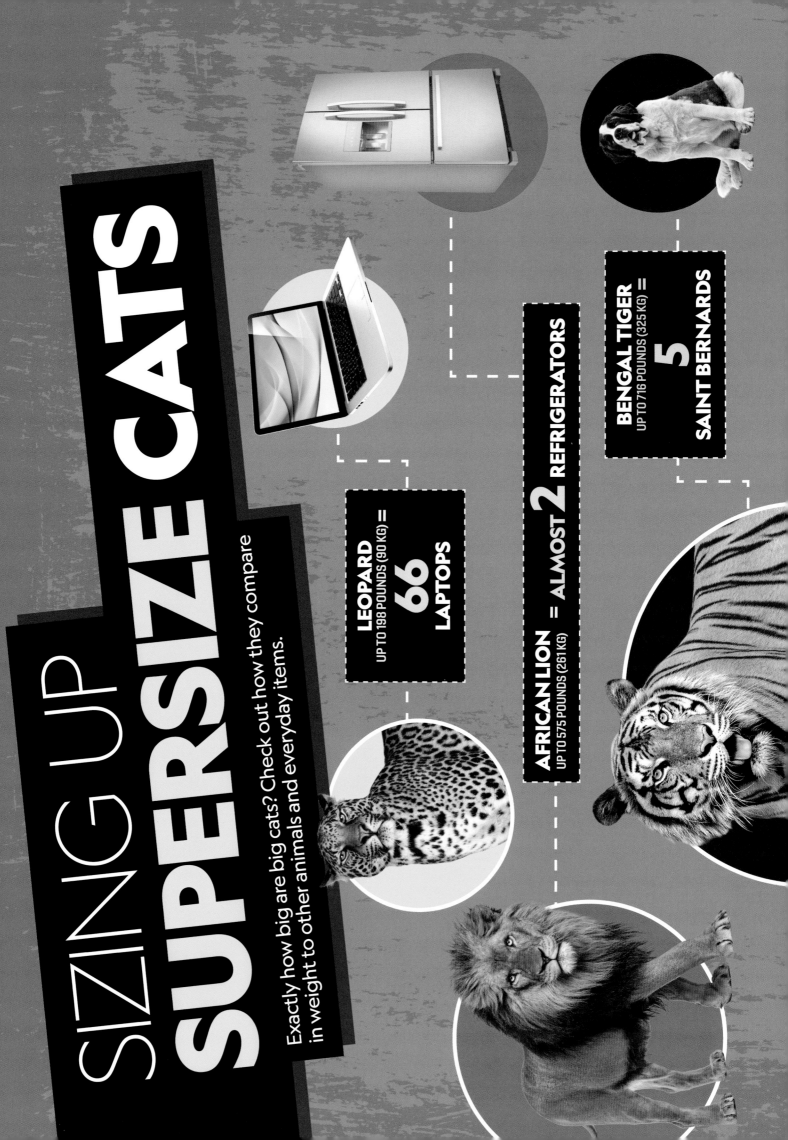

LEOPARD
UP TO 198 POUNDS (90 KG) =

66
LAPTOPS

AFRICAN LION
UP TO 575 POUNDS (261 KG) = ALMOST **2** REFRIGERATORS

BENGAL TIGER
UP TO 716 POUNDS (325 KG) =

5
SAINT BERNARDS

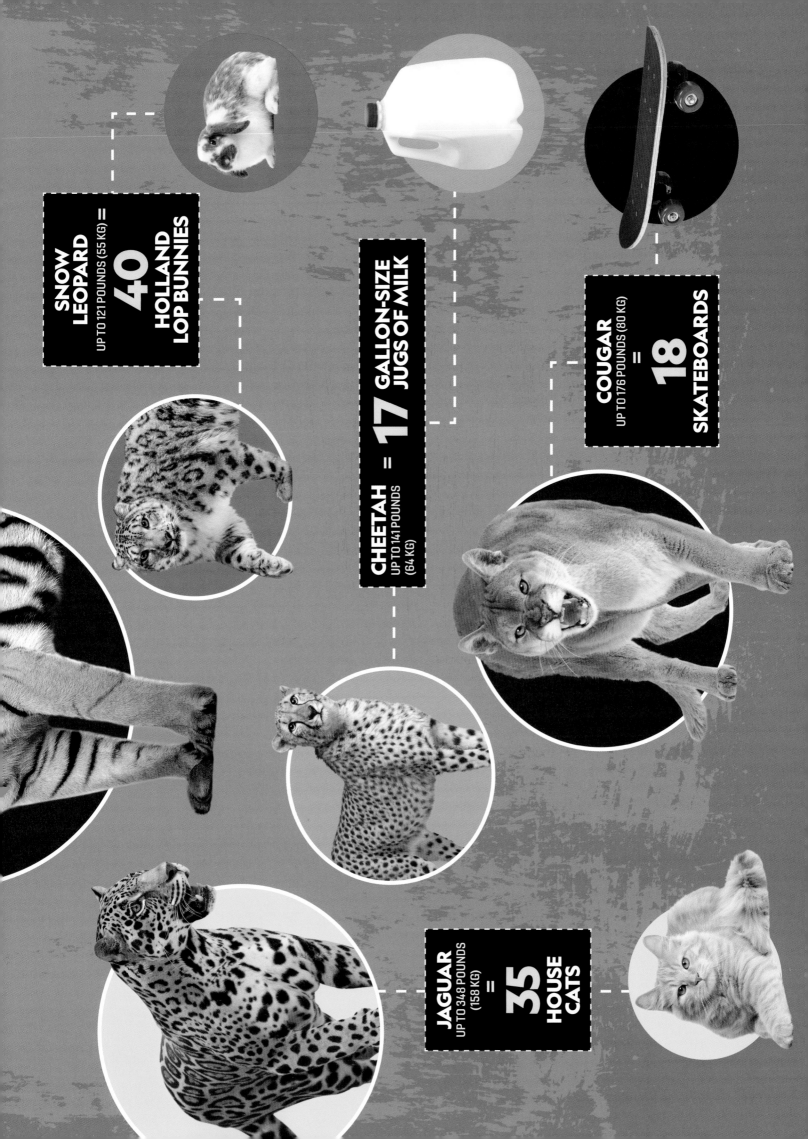

SNOW LEOPARD
UP TO 121 POUNDS (55 KG) =
40
HOLLAND LOP BUNNIES

CHEETAH = **17** GALLON-SIZE JUGS OF MILK
UP TO 141 POUNDS (64 KG)

COUGAR
UP TO 176 POUNDS (80 KG)
=
18
SKATEBOARDS

JAGUAR
UP TO 348 POUNDS (158 KG)
=
35
HOUSE CATS

WINTER'S TALE

THE SECRET LIVES OF SNOW LEOPARDS

MY SNOW LEOPARD STORY WAS THE HARDEST THING I'VE EVER DONE.
Up until then I was a jungle guy—I'd always photographed in hot, humid rainforests. It was a shock to land in India's Himalayan mountains in the heart of winter and work in crazy, extreme cold.

Preparing for an assignment is always intense—figuring out where to work, who to work with, and what equipment I'll need. But this was going to be a four-month expedition, camping at high altitude in the wilderness, so I had to bring extra equipment. If anything broke, we would have no way to fix or replace it. We also needed a medical kit—there would be no doctors! There were 10 of us: biologists, local experts from Snow Leopard Conservancy India Trust, three assistants, and a cook. I had to outfit an entire camp with warm clothing, tents, cots, sleeping bags, and food.

We walked for half a day to our first campsite in Hemis National Park. It took 20 packhorses three days, going back and forth, to ferry our gear. The site was above the tree line at 15,000 feet (4,570 m). It looked like the moon: rocky, dusty, and barren. The air was so thin that after walking just a few steps I had to stop, panting. I slept fully clothed inside three sleeping bags and wore two hats. I put a hot-water bottle on my feet; by morning it was frozen solid. It went down to 50° below zero Fahrenheit (-46°C) on the coldest nights!

Somehow I had to come home with photographs of a cat that is so elusive it is nicknamed the "ghost cat of the Himalaya."

On my second day there, we spotted two snow leopards through binoculars, tiny dots moving on a faraway peak. That gave me hope that I'd be successful. I never saw one again.

I knew that the only way to photograph the cats was with camera traps. Snow leopards roam massive territories, but, luckily, they have regular habits. Every week or two, they walked the same route along ridges or at the bottom of steep cliffs, scratching or spraying to mark their territory—and that's where I installed cameras. Any animal that walked by and broke the invisible infrared beam of light from the transmitter fired the camera.

I started getting pictures. Some were good. Others were just part of a cat—or the equipment didn't work well in the extreme cold and I missed a shot. Sometimes there were pictures of rabbits or blue sheep—or nothing at all.

It was exhausting, but in the end, it was all worthwhile. After months of grueling work, a cat wandered past my camera at night, dusted white by the falling snow, and marked on a big rock. The photo was seen by people around the world, showing them the majesty of this cat. Many people donated money to support snow leopard conservation. It's what I try to do in my work: create images that make people care about wildlife and help protect my wild subjects.

A cheetah stalks through tall grass in the Phinda Private Game Reserve, in South Africa.

CHAPTER TWO

BIG CATS INSIDE AND OUT

>>> BIG CATS HAVE IT ALL. They are fierce, powerful, and highly successful predators. Their coloring, stripes, and spots allow them to stalk their homelands almost invisibly. The cats use their keen senses to locate prey—even in the dark. Then they wait patiently, concentrating on the animal's every move, until the moment they charge, claws out and mouths open.

These cats are perfectly evolved, fearsome hunters. They're some of the animal kingdom's superheroes, the top predators in every ecosystem they inhabit. Get ready to get up close with big cats—and with their small- and medium-size cousins, too!

SEEING SPOTS (AND STRIPES)

>>> FOUR BIG CATS ARE KNOWN FOR THEIR MAG-NIFICENT SPOTTED COATS: LEOPARDS, JAGUARS, SNOW LEOPARDS, AND CHEETAHS. For tigers, it's all about stripes. Their striped coats not only are beautiful, but they also turn these cats into masters of disguise, allowing them to blend into the landscape. Camouflage is important because the sneak attack is a big cat's greatest hunting weapon, and it's pretty hard to take prey by surprise if they can see you coming! Spots or stripes, there's much more to these big cats' coats than meets the eye.

Tiger

Tigers don't just have striped fur—**THEIR SKIN IS ALSO STRIPED!** And every tiger's stripe pattern is unique, just like a human fingerprint.

STEALTH WITH STRIPES

With its orange coat and distinctive stripes, how does a tiger disappear into tall grasses or shadowy forests? The black slashes of its stripes help break up the outline of its body, making it hard to spot in jungles or grass-lands either during the day or under the moonlight. Since tigers often hunt in darkness, the stripes look like shadows to unsuspecting prey.

GETTING SPOTTED

Lions and cougars are the only big cats without spots or stripes—but not their babies! Cougar kittens are born with spots and rings around their tails. Lion cubs are covered in brown spots, or rosettes, that are similar to a leopard's. Researchers believe that this coat pattern may have camouflaged lions' ancestors that lived in forests long ago. But the spots still protect cubs today, keeping them hidden while they're young and helpless. They fade as the cats reach adulthood, but some lionesses have faint spots on their legs and bellies for life.

Lion cub

ABOUT 2,000 INKY BLACK SPOTS dapple a cheetah's body—everywhere except its stomach.

Cheetah

Snow leopard

SEASONAL SPOTS

A snow leopard's coat changes to fit the season. In winter, it gets lighter for better camouflage against the snow. In summer, its fur changes to yellowish gray to help the cat camouflage in the dusty hillsides and rocky outcroppings of the Central Asian mountains where it roams.

POWERFUL PAWS

A wild cat's paws are among its most important survival tools.

Well-Padded

Cats can walk almost silently as they prowl after unsuspecting prey. The soft, spongy pads on the bottoms of their feet give them secret stealth. They literally tiptoe: When they step, only their toes touch the ground, which also helps them run fast.

Sweaty Paws

On a hot day, cats cool down by sweating through their paws. They also perspire when they're scared or nervous: Adrenaline and other fight-or-flight hormones trigger cats' sweat glands.

A male tiger in India's Bandhavgarh Tiger Reserve stalks his territory.

HIGH-TECH PAWS

A cat's paws are one of the most sensitive parts of its body and act as highly tuned sensors. Because its paw pads are loaded with nerve endings, a cat can feel vibrations from approaching or fleeing animals. Cat paws are also extremely flexible: They can swivel inward and allow cats to sink their claws into trees.

Lion

A big cat's paw print is called a **PUGMARK.**

Snow leopard

Weatherproof

Snow leopards have evolved extra-large paws to navigate their steep, craggy Himalayan homeland in the wintertime. Their paws are like snowshoes: They are super wide, which helps distribute the cats' body weight so they can walk on top of the snow. Fur cushions the bottom of their paws so they can scramble over sharp rocks without ripping up their feet. Their paw pads also act as shock absorbers.

A Mighty Blow

A big cat's paw is like a club. One powerful strike from a lion's paw can crush a hyena or knock a buffalo down to the ground. A tiger can break an animal's neck with a single blow.

Young tigers play-fight.

CLAWS OUT

Big cats' razor-sharp claws aren't just for hunting.

A lion's claws grip prey.

>>> **MOST BIG CATS' CLAWS ARE LONG, THICK, HOOKED—AND DEADLY.** Cats use them to grab hold of prey or scramble up trees. They act as important multipurpose tools that help these cats survive.

Secret Weapon

A big cat's claws are normally invisible, retracted inside a protective sheath in its paws. When their claws are drawn in, cats can move around noiselessly. But like a secret weapon, cats can extend their claws in a flash to snag and hold on to prey or to defend themselves. Because claws are usually pulled back, they stay sharp. Cheetahs are the exception. They have short, blunt claws that are semi-retractable—similar to a dog's—and work like cleats, gripping the ground as they run.

A Siberian tiger's curved claws are four inches (10 cm) long— **THAT'S LONGER THAN A CRAYON!**

A tiger's scratch marks on a tree trunk in India

Tigers can climb trees. But they can only **CRAWL DOWN BACKWARD OR JUMP DOWN** because of their large size and weight and the shape of their claws. This makes them some of the most challenged climbers among the big cats.

Scratch Marks the Spot

Claws have another important function: scratching! Tigers use trees like giant scratching posts, etching deep marks into the bark. This sharpens their claws, but it also sends messages to other cats. The scratches are a kind of calling card to help the solitary cats find a mate. It's also a way to mark territory or advertise their presence, helping them avoid surprise encounters and fights that could prove fatal.

Bonus Claw

Most cats have 18 claws: five on each of their front paws and four on each of their back paws. The extra ones up front, the dew claws, sit higher on their legs and don't touch the ground. The dew claws work like a spiky thumb, helping cats latch on to their prey.

African lion cubs play with a large piece of elephant dung.

A TALE OF TAILS

A cat's tail helps this feline hunt and send messages to other cats.

A leopard surveys the ground from a high limb.

A mother leopard **SWISHES HER WHITE-TIPPED TAIL** to tell her cubs to **BE QUIET** when she's approaching prey.

Balancing Act

Just as a tightrope walker uses a pole to keep balanced on a high wire, cats use their tails to steady themselves when running after—or jumping on—their prey. Tree-climbing cats, including leopards and jaguars, also use their tails for balance when walking along branches.

Cheetah

A female lion and her cub

Built-In Rudder

When a cheetah sprints at full speed in pursuit of an animal, the chase is rarely run in a straight line. The prey twists, turns, and zigzags to try to escape from this extremely fast cat. But cheetahs stick with them by "steering" with their long tails—which can be more than 2.5 feet (0.8 m) long. A superlong tail also helps a snow leopard streak down steep, rocky mountainsides after a blue sheep or other prey without falling.

Follow Me!

Lions are the only cats with a tuft at the end of their tails. Mother lions use their black tasseled tails like a flag. They raise their tails up high to lead their cubs through the tall grasses of the African savanna. It's also a communication tool: Lions signal other members of the pride and give directions or commands with a flick of their tails.

Mood Swing

Humans aren't the only ones that communicate with body language. Cats move their tails to express their emotions and convey their mood. If a cat is twitching or whipping its tail back and forth, it's agitated and could be aggressive. If its tail is tucked between its legs, the cat may be feeling nervous or submissive. But if a cat is slowly waving its tail, beware: It's focused on something, possibly ready to spring. And if its tail is still, the cat is probably relaxed.

A family of cheetahs

SINK YOUR TEETH INTO THIS!

Big cats can take down large prey with a single bite.

Strongest Bite

The jaguar's mighty jaws are so strong that this cat can easily crunch through its prey's skull, bite through bones, crack open turtle shells, and pierce the thick leathery skin of a caiman (a cousin of the crocodile). Its bite is powered by exceptionally strong jaw muscles. While tigers have a more powerful bite, jaguars have the strongest bite force, relative to their size, of any large cat.

>>> WHEN THESE SKILLED HUNTERS ATTACK, THEY MUST QUICKLY OVERCOME THEIR PREY TO SNARE A MEAL—AND TO AVOID INJURY FROM HORNS, TEETH, AND HOOVES. They subdue their prey by clamping down on its throat, skull, or the back of its neck. This requires sharp, saberlike canine teeth and powerful jaws.

A jaguar pulls a caiman from a river in the Pantanal, in central Brazil.

Lion

What Big Teeth You Have!

A lion's sharp, massive canine teeth measure up to four inches (10 cm) long. These four daggerlike teeth grab and hold on to prey. Its other teeth finish the job. The lion's incisors, or small front teeth, grip and tear meat, picking off small scraps. Its back teeth are the sharpest, shearing away meat that the cat then swallows whole, without chewing. With jaws that can open 11 inches (28 cm) wide, lions have one of the largest bites in the animal kingdom!

Cheetah

What Small Teeth You Have!

Because cheetahs rely on speed, and a sprinting chase requires a lot of oxygen, they have unusually large nasal passages. This leaves little space in the cat's small, lightweight skull for teeth. Cheetahs evolved to have small canine teeth and kill by strangling their prey: They clamp down and hold on. These cats don't need big teeth to be great hunters.

"While working in India, I watched in awe as a big male tiger stalked an Asian elephant herd for two hours. He stayed downwind, where they couldn't smell him. He crept silently through the tall grass, his stripes acting as the perfect invisibility cloak. The adult elephants circled the calves when they sensed the tiger's presence, facing outward to defend them. The tiger retreated, napped, and tried again and again. But after four unsuccessful attempts, he sauntered off."

—Steve Winter

53

NOSING AROUND

Big cats have an amazing sense of smell.

>>> A BIG CAT'S SENSE OF SMELL IS ABOUT 100 TIMES STRONGER THAN A HUMAN'S. That's because it doesn't use just its nose to catch a scent.

A Second Nose

A cat has a "second nose," known as Jacobson's organ, which is made up of two fluid-filled sacs above the roof of its mouth. Its job is to detect scent chemicals, or pheromones, left behind by other cats. To do this, a cat breathes in through its mouth and curls its lip in a grimace called the flehmen response. When the Jacobson's organ detects chemical cat messages, it sends that information via nerves to the cat's brain. The cat may learn that an intruder is in its territory—or that another cat is looking for a mate!

Lion

A BREATH OF WARM AIR

Can you imagine surviving outdoors in the winter, living high in the mountains in sub-zero temperatures like a snow leopard? Simply breathing is one way this cat keeps warm. Its large nostrils and oversize nasal cavity act like a little heater, warming frigid air before it reaches the cat's lungs.

Snow leopard

IN THEIR SIGHTS

Big cats use their piercing gaze to target prey.

A Predator's Pupils

Each of the seven big cats has rounded pupils, while their smaller cat cousins have vertical, slit-shaped pupils. Scientists discovered that pupil shape is linked to an animal's lifestyle. It seems that small ambush predators that are active both day and night (and are closer to the ground) have slit-shaped pupils. Larger predators—including big cats—that chase down their prey have round pupils.

Bengal tiger

Most big cats have yellow or golden eyes. **SNOW LEOPARDS ARE AN EXCEPTION.** They have blue, gray, or green eyes.

Snow leopard

Night-Light

Since most big cats are on the prowl at dawn and dusk, they have spectacular night vision. A lion can see in the dark about six times better than you can. That's because its big eyes are packed with photoreceptor cells that pick up light as it comes in. Then a special lining of reflecting cells behind the retina shines light back onto these light-sensitive photoreceptor cells. This gives the cat the ability to see in near darkness and makes its eyes seem to glow in the dark.

Forward Focus

Cats' eyes are set far apart, giving them a wide view. But they still face forward, which means cats have "binocular vision" to pinpoint their prey. Cats see in muted color—not the same rich hues that humans see. But unlike people, these top-notch predators don't have to blink to keep their eyes moist, so they can hold their gaze on moving prey for a long time.

BRING ON THE SUN

While most big cats rest during the heat of the day, cheetahs hunt. Their huge, high-set eyes give them a wide-angle view, and with their keen eyesight, they can spot an impala or other prey up to two miles (3.2 km) away. While their daytime vision is excellent, they don't see as well in the dark as nighttime hunters do.

Cheetah

ALL EARS

Big cats' highly tuned ears act like little satellite dishes that pick up the tiniest sounds.

Female leopard

Listen Up!

Big cats can swivel their ears up to 180 degrees to pinpoint where a sound is coming from. Dozens of muscles allow them to turn their ears in different directions. Their ears can also turn independently of each other. Super hearing helps cats find their next meal, even in the dark, and enables them to hear the squeals of their cubs or other big cats calling in the distance.

Can You Hear That?

A cat's hearing is a marvel of engineering. Lions can hear their prey from a mile (1.6 km) away. And tigers can hear things that humans can't. They make low-frequency sounds (that are inaudible to us) to warn rivals or to attract a mate. Researchers discovered that these sounds travel farther than the high-frequency ones we can hear. In Indonesia, hunters once believed that a tiger's hearing was so sharp that the cat could hear the wind whistling through human hairs—so the hunters shaved off all their body hair!

Male lion

Eye Spy

Tigers have white spots, or "flashes," on the back of their ears that could be mistaken for eyes. Scientists aren't exactly sure of their purpose, but one theory is that these "false eyes" may fool prey. They may also scare away potential attackers—including other tigers that might want to jump them from behind. When threatened, tigers twist their ears forward, so displaying these markings may be an act of aggression. Another theory is that the markings send signals to other tigers.

Tiger

HEAR ME ROAR!

The "roaring cats"—lions, tigers, leopards, and jaguars—make themselves heard.

Jaguar

It Might Get Loud

Roaring is all about the larynx. This organ, found at the top of the throat, houses the voice box, which allows both humans and animals to make sounds. It takes a large voice box to belt out deep, throaty roars. But the four "roaring cats" have an extra advantage: They have specially shaped vocal cords. In most animals, the vocal cords are triangular, but in these cats they are square and flat. This difference makes the roaring cats the opera singers of the cat kingdom: They can produce louder calls with less lung pressure.

Hello!

Tigers, leopards, snow leopards, and jaguars chuff when saying a friendly hello to another cat at mating time or as a greeting when a mom returns home to her cubs. It's a gentle snort made by blowing through their noses while their mouths are closed.

Jaguar cub with mother

Loudmouths

Researchers discovered that a lion's roar is similar to a human baby's cry—though a lion's roar is at a much lower pitch. One scientist found out why they are similar: Both adult lions and human babies have loose and gel-like vocal cords that vibrate irregularly, making their roars and cries sound rough. A baby cries to voice a need for help. A lion roars to get attention, too, but mainly to warn intruders, "This is my territory, get out of here!"

Female lion

PURR-FECTLY HAPPY NOT TO ROAR

The big cats that can't roar do something the others can't: They purr! But how? The ability to purr centers around the hyoid bone, which sits in a cat's throat and supports its larynx and tongue. In cheetahs, cougars, and snow leopards, this bone is rigid. When the larynx vibrates, the hyoid bone creates a low rumble, or purr, that continues while the cat breathes in and out. In the roaring cats, this bone is flexible, so they can't purr.

Cheetahs touch noses to greet each other.

BUILT FOR SPEED

A cheetah's anatomy makes it the fastest land animal on Earth.

>>> CHEETAHS ARE SMALLER THAN THE LIONS AND LEOPARDS THEY LIVE BESIDE ON THE AFRICAN GRASSLANDS, BUT THEY ARE SO MUCH FASTER! Cheetahs are the number one speed racer among cats. They can hit an unbelievable 70 miles an hour (113 km/h) in just over three seconds. These sprinters can only chase in short bursts; they are not long-distance runners.

Sure-Footed

At full speed, a cheetah's hind legs and front legs overlap underneath its body, thrusting it forward, with extra traction from special foot pads that act like tire treads. At two points in its stride, all four feet are extended, and the cat's body is completely off the ground. Cheetahs can cover up to 21 feet (6.4 m) with one stride, powered by serious muscles: Its leg and back muscles make up half of its body weight.

ON YOUR MARK ...

If all seven big cats were in a race, in what order would they cross the finish line?

	0 mph	10 mph
CHEETAH: 70 miles an hour (113 km/h)		
COUGAR: 50 miles an hour (80 km/h)		
JAGUAR: 40 miles an hour (64 km/h)		
SNOW LEOPARD: 40 miles an hour (64 km/h)		
LION: 37 miles an hour (60 km/h)		
LEOPARD: 37 miles an hour (60 km/h)		
TIGER: 35 miles an hour (56 km/h)		

Miles an hour for short bursts at maximum speed

Bendy Back

The cheetah has a uniquely long, flexible spine. Unlike a racehorse's spine, which stays relatively flat when the horse is galloping, a cheetah's spine coils and uncoils like a metal spring when the cat runs. This allows its shoulders and hips to swing through arcs, which lengthens its stride and enables it to cover more ground more quickly.

Eye on the Game

When a cheetah is sprinting after an animal at breakneck speed, its legs are a spinning blur. But its head is perfectly still, and its eyes remain focused on its prize.

Cheetahs can speed up or slow down by nine miles an hour (14 km/h) **IN ONE STRIDE.**

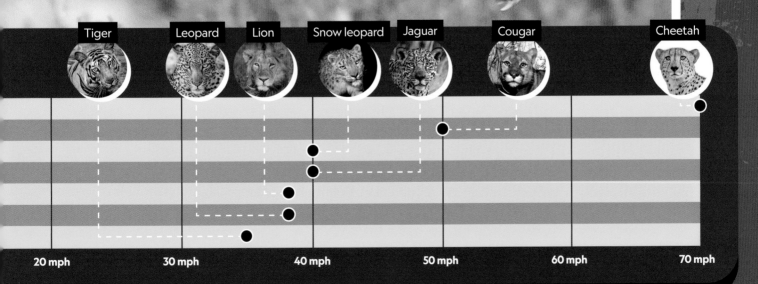

| Tiger | Leopard | Lion | Snow leopard | Jaguar | Cougar | Cheetah |

| 20 mph | 30 mph | 40 mph | 50 mph | 60 mph | 70 mph |

ULTIMATE CLIMBERS

Leopards and snow leopards could both win a climbing contest by leaps and bounds. In a side-by-side comparison, these big cats are evenly matched—but in very different ways.

LEOPARDS

Leopards are natural-born tree climbers: Their strong necks, shoulders, and jaws allow them to carry animals heavier than they are straight up a tree. Digging in with their sharp claws, they easily climb back down, headfirst.

Leopards lose many of their hard-won meals to fierce competitors—lions, hyenas, and wild dogs. One of the only ways to protect their food is to move the carcass high up onto a tree branch as soon as they kill the animal. Lions aren't great climbers, and hyenas and wild dogs can only howl and bark at leopards from the ground, waiting for a few scraps of meat to fall. Scientists who study leopards at Sabi Sands Game Reserve in South Africa learned that the leopards using this strategy were 67 percent less likely to have their meals stolen. They found that leopards choose their spot carefully if they have time, draping their kill in a tree that has a good fork or a sturdy branch. But if they're being chased, they bolt up the nearest tree.

SNOW LEOPARDS

Snow leopards are mountain-climbing adventurers in their rocky Himalayan and Central Asian homeland. They live at the highest altitude of any cat—up to 18,000 feet (5,500 m). They're perfectly adapted for heart-pumping sprints, jumping between rocks and across huge chasms to catch prey. At those heights, there is little oxygen. Their wide nasal passages and large chests help them breathe deeply. They also have more red blood cells than other big cats do to carry oxygen throughout their bodies.

Their powerful hind legs—which are longer than their front ones—help make snow leopards the mighty leapers they are. Their broad chests also help absorb the impact of their nearly vertical leaps on mountain slopes. Snow leopards can jump 45 feet (14 m) in a single bound—farther than any other big cat!

BIG—BUT NOT "BIG"—CATS

Meet some medium-size predators whose hunting skills mimic those of their big cat cousins.

>>> MOST OF THE PLANET'S WILD CATS—34 OUT OF THE 41 SPECIES—ARE MIDSIZE OR SMALL. The tiniest one, the rusty-spotted cat, which lives in Asia, weighs about half as much as your pet cat—around four pounds (2 kg)! Some of these smaller species have never been studied by field biologists, so we know very little about them. With ongoing DNA studies, the cat family may continue to grow as scientists identify distinctly different new members. Though each species has its own habits, these cats have the same basic body structure and the same number of teeth and bones as both big cats and house cats.

Lynx

SCIENTIFIC NAME: *Lynx* spp.

WEIGHT: Up to 65 pounds (30 kg)

RANGE: North America, Europe, and Asia

Freezing cold weather and deep snow are no problem for the lynx. With their bushy fur and oversize paws, these cats are built for harsh, frigid winters in the northern forests of North America, Europe, and Asia where they live. Their big paws help them race atop deep snow to catch the swift animals that are their favorite prey, the snowshoe hare and blue sheep. They have super senses, too: Spiky tufts on their ears act as hearing aids, amplifying the sound of nearby animals. And with their eaglelike eyesight, they can spot a mouse from almost a football field away!

Caracal

SCIENTIFIC NAME:	*Caracal caracal*
WEIGHT:	Up to 44 pounds (20 kg)
RANGE:	Middle East, Africa, Central Asia, and India

Caracals may not be big cats, but they can jump like them. These sleek, reddish gold cats are small—just two feet (0.6 m) tall—but they've been filmed leaping over a nine-foot (2.7-m) fence to go after sheep. They're fast, acrobatic, and stealthy. Their cushioned foot pads allow them to sneak up on rabbits, rodents, birds, and even gazelles. But a caracal's most striking feature is the signature long, black tufts on top of its pointy ears. Scientists aren't sure about their purpose. These tufts may help keep flies out of its face or act as camouflage by breaking up the outline of its head amid tall grass. This cat sometimes twitches its ear tufts to communicate with other caracals.

Serval

SCIENTIFIC NAME:	*Leptailurus serval*
WEIGHT:	Up to 40 pounds (18 kg)
RANGE:	Sub-Saharan Africa

The "giraffe cat"—the serval—is perfectly suited to pounce on prey in the African grasslands where it lives. This cat has extra-long legs and an elongated neck and can vault itself 12 feet (4 m) into the air to grab a low-flying bird! With extraordinarily large, oval-shaped ears, a serval can detect the presence of any animal scurrying about. (If you had ears like a serval, they would be the size of dinner plates!)

Clouded Leopard

SCIENTIFIC NAME:	*Neofelis nebulosa*
WEIGHT:	Up to 55 pounds (25 kg)
RANGE:	Asia

Rarely seen, clouded leopards are one of the most secretive cats. They roam from the cloud forests of Borneo north to the foothills of Nepal's Himalaya. As one of the most ancient cat species, they're the closest relative to the big cats. But clouded leopards are not actually a type of leopard.

These cats are one of the few animals that can climb down trees headfirst. Their specialized anklebones rotate to allow them to do this, and their sharp claws and special foot pads grip the bark. They can even hang upside down from branches!

SMALL AND MIGHTY

These petite predators share big cats' survival instincts.

Rusty-Spotted Cat

SCIENTIFIC NAME: *Prionailurus rubiginosus*

WEIGHT: Up to 3.5 pounds (1.6 kg)

RANGE: India, Sri Lanka

The rusty-spotted cat is the world's smallest wild cat, but it has a reputation for being especially fierce. This little cat has short legs, big eyes, and long stripes that extend onto its head. It mostly lives in forests, on grasslands, or near villages, sometimes moving into abandoned houses or tea plantations. Like many other small cats, it thrives on rodents and chickens that live near humans.

Rusty-spotted cat

Pallas's Cat

SCIENTIFIC NAME: *Otocolobus manul*

WEIGHT: Up to 10 pounds (4.5 kg)

RANGE: Central Asia

The Pallas's cat—also known as a manul or rock wildcat—has amber eyes and short ears. It's so fluffy that it almost looks round. It became an internet star because of its now famous grumpy expression. It needs its megathick coat to survive freezing winters in Central Asia. This tiny ambush predator tends to wait until prey wanders close enough before pouncing. It's a poor runner, so when threatened, it freezes and flattens itself to the ground to hide.

Marbled Cat

SCIENTIFIC NAME: *Pardofelis marmorata*

WEIGHT: Up to 11 pounds (5 kg)

RANGE: Southeast Asia

This cat gets its name from its coat's dappled, or marbled, pattern. Its tail is extraordinarily long, longer than the rest of its body. Not much is known about its behavior, but scientists think its tail acts as a counterbalance when the cat is up in the trees of Southeast Asia's tropical forests. The marbled cat is believed to be diurnal—awake and hunting during the daytime.

Jaguarundi

SCIENTIFIC NAME: *Herpailurus yagouaroundi*

WEIGHT: Up to 15 pounds (7 kg)

RANGE: Parts of Mexico, Central America, and South America

The jaguarundi's closest relative is the cougar, but you probably wouldn't guess that by looking at it. In fact, from a distance you might mistake the jaguarundi, with its long, slender body, narrow head, and little ears, for a type of otter or weasel. Like the cheetah, it can't retract its claws completely. Jaguarundis live in all kinds of habitats and eat many kinds of small animals. Their voices have quite a range, too—they purr, whistle, chatter, and even chirp like a bird!

House cats share a branch of their family tree with **BLACK-FOOTED CATS,** jungle cats, and two other small wild cats.

WINTER'S TALE

TREE-CLIMBING LIONS

I LOVE WORKING IN AFRICA. EACH DAY IS FILLED WITH MAGICAL ENCOUNTERS. A massive herd of zebras and wildebeests. A giraffe extending its impossibly long neck to munch leaves from a tall branch. Birds with iridescent turquoise feathers. Rhinos! Elephants! Cheetahs!

And lions in trees?

Photographing tree-climbing lions was a truly otherworldly assignment. This pride was nestled deep inside Queen Elizabeth National Park in Uganda. They looked no different than other African lions, except the males had black manes. But they behaved differently. We often saw six or seven of them lounging lazily on the boughs of a tree.

I spent a month there, working with Alex Braczkowski, a big cat biologist and filmmaker who was studying these cats and filming their rare and mysterious behavior for a documentary. He told me that lions occasionally climb trees in other parts of Africa. But these cats are among the few that spend substantial amounts of time on high. It might be a family tradition that cubs learn by watching the adults and then copying their behavior. It's part of their culture.

They're not the best climbers, but that didn't stop these cats. Lions aren't built like the sleek, agile leopards that bound easily among branches; lions are bulkier, heavier, and much slower and more cautious in a tree. Sometimes the cats seemed nervous about coming down, going headfirst, and then turning around to lower themselves tail first, trying different options before finally reaching the ground.

Why do they climb? Some scientists claim that the cats are escaping insects that infest the savanna during the rainy season—especially the biting tsetse flies. Others think they're trying to escape the scorching daytime heat, catching a breeze while they rest in the shade. A lofty limb can also act as an observation tower for the lions' next hunt, offering a cool view of potential prey. And who knows, they may also climb for fun, especially the young lions.

Braczkowski counted 71 lions living in the park in different groups. The prides are smaller than they were decades ago, but the group we were documenting was a small miracle: Their numbers had doubled in this part of the park.

A smaller pride can't easily hunt big animals like African buffalo. Small, reddish brown kob antelope are their favored meal. But people also eat kob. That leaves less prey for lions, forcing them to range farther to find food—and they sometimes wander into a village to take down a cow or goat. This is a devastating loss for a family that has just a few animals. Some people retaliate by poisoning lions.

But there are usually solutions for even the most complicated problems. Conservationists are trying to raise funds to build predator-proof enclosures and to pay villagers for lost livestock. They'd also like to fit the cats with GPS collars so they can track them, and rangers can then warn local people when the animals are nearby. These measures will help people live with lions.

CHAPTER THREE

WHEN BIG CATS WERE CUBS

≫ **BIG CATS ARE BORN TINY, BLIND, AND WITHOUT TEETH.** They are completely dependent on their mother. But once their eyes open—and before they grow up and must hunt for their own food and defend their territory—the cubs get to kick up their paws and have fun. They spend their days swatting, biting, pouncing on, and chasing their brothers and sisters. This isn't just fun and games: They're practicing skills they'll need to survive as *big* big cats! Cubs stay with their mother for one to two years before heading off on their own. But some are forever homebodies, like female lions that stay with their pride for life. Let's peek into the lives of big cat cubs!

Cheetah cubs play in the savanna in South Africa.

MOMMY AND ME

All big cat babies stick close to mom.

Cheetah cubs cuddle with their mother.

Bonding Time

A cougar mother births up to five babies at once. (Big cats can have anywhere from one to eight cubs.) She nestles with her newborns in their den for about 10 days, communicating with them by purring—almost constantly! All big cat moms bond with their babies by licking them from head to tail, but it's also a bath. Moms and cubs get cheeky, too: Rubbing faces, especially along the cheeks, is scent-marking, which makes it easy to keep track of each other.

Food First

Big cat moms are pregnant for three to four months. At birth, cougars weigh about a pound (0.4 kg); tigers weigh about 3.5 pounds (1.6 kg). For the first few weeks of life, helpless big cat cubs require their mother's constant protection and warmth; their eyes don't open until they're seven to 14 days old. They need to nurse constantly to survive. Early on, they double their weight almost every week. But mothers need to eat, too, so they must leave to go hunting. Alone, the cubs are vulnerable to all kinds of predators. To keep them safe, a mother conceals them in a secret, cozy den that's hidden in tall grass, a rocky crevice, or a cave. Camouflage helps: Even cats with plain coats, like lions and cheetahs, are born with spots that help keep them hidden.

What a Mouthful

What better way to transport a tiny wriggling cub than by the scruff of its neck? Even house cats do it! If a mother cat senses danger, she tenderly carries her babies, one by one, in her mouth to a new den. This motherly move triggers a natural reflex: The baby goes limp, and its legs curl up for more streamlined carrying.

A leopard mother carries her cub.

Learning in Action

Big cats are carnivores: They eat meat. They must hunt to survive, and cubs begin training when they're just a few months old. Their mothers bring wounded prey back to the den, and the cubs chase and pounce on it. The siblings wrestle and spring on anything that moves, from a leaf or an insect to their sister's or brother's waving tail. Practice-hunting helps cubs hone their skills until they're big enough to go out on hunts with their mother or the pride. At about six weeks old, cheetahs are the youngest big cat to venture from the den. Because cheetahs roam a wide territory to find food, mothers have to bring their cubs along.

Family Get-Togethers

Lions are the only social big cat. They live in groups called prides, and each generation of cubs has nearly the same birthday. The females, which are often related, give birth around the same time. Then they jointly care for the babies as one big family. And here's something else to make you feel warm and fuzzy: A leopard cub is so bonded with its mom that even after it has left home and settled into its own territory, it may return for a brief family reunion.

Back Off!

Don't mess with a mother big cat! Her number one job is to protect her cubs. That means she's a fighter. She must fend off male cats that might attack them, as well as wolves, hyenas, or even dogs or snakes that could kill her babies. Finding a good hideout, like a hidden cave or a camouflaged nest in tall grass, is a top priority.

A cheetah mother snarls a warning at a pair of male cheetahs to stay away from her cubs.

A lion pride

Saying Goodbye

Most big cats leave their families and strike out on their own when they are 18 months to two years old—except for lions and cheetahs. Female lions stay with their pride. As for cheetahs, moms leave their cubs when they're a year and a half old. The siblings won't split up for another six months. The young females leave first, but the males often continue to live and hunt together in a group called a coalition.

FAMILY PRIDE

All the other big cats are solitary, but lions live in structured communities.

A lion and lioness lounge in the dry savanna grass in South Africa.

Lion King

A pride can be tiny or huge, with just three cats or up to 40. But regardless of the number, they're ruled by one dominant male. Lionesses and their young make up most of the group: Females usually stay for life. A big pride may include a few other males, but most male cubs are gone by their second birthday. They head off to try to start their own pride, usually by taking over another one!

The main job of the "lion king" is to defend his family's territory. His roars—which can echo over five miles (8 km)—along with scratches and scent markings, let other lions know that he rules the area. He also fends off other males that try to move in on his turf.

LION YAWNS ARE CONTAGIOUS! If one lion in a pride yawns, others often will, too.

Equal Footing

Talk about sisterhood! Recent studies found that, unlike other animal societies, lionesses lack a hierarchy: They all have equal power in the pride. They are usually all related—grandmothers, mothers, daughters, sisters, and aunts—and they do most of the hunting.

Daycare Duty

Lionesses in a pride are also partners in raising, protecting, and feeding cubs. Each of them gives birth in their own den at nearly the same time. They care for their babies for the first four to six weeks, and then they all regroup. The females become one big parenting team, sharing cubsitting duties and sometimes even suckling hungry cubs that are not their own.

Lionesses

Lionesses with their pride

A lioness pride takes down an African buffalo in Botswana, Africa.

Hunters in Training

Working together, lions can take down massive prey, including animals like zebras or wildebeests that are much larger and heavier than they are. Lion cubs spend most of their first year watching how it's done, but at 15 or 16 months old, they are big enough to join in—and even capture prey!

CAT SCHOOL

Big cat cubs have a lot of skills to master during their first two years of life.

Role Models

When lion cubs leave the den and join the pride, the lionesses become their role models. They show cubs the ropes, pointing out everything from the best shady spots to rest to the best meat to eat on a kill. At about two years old, the young adult cats officially graduate from "cat school."

A lion mom instructs her cub on the finer points of hunting.

Skill Work

When baby big cats run, climb, and wrestle, it's more than just playtime. They're in training, like athletes, developing the strength, coordination, and strategies they'll need to survive as effective hunters.

Cheetahs clamber up low trees to survey the landscape, so cubs need good climbing skills.

Leopard cub

High Achievers

Learning to climb trees is high on the list of lessons for a leopard cub. A lofty limb is a safe place for leopards to escape from lions and other predators, as well as a safe place to stash their kill.

A lioness teaches her cubs to hunt.

Practice Makes Perfect

Lion cubs get special instruction when they become hunters-in-training. Sometimes, several adults give a group lesson. They capture a smaller animal, like an impala, which they wound but don't kill. Then they surround it so it can't escape and let the cubs practice attacking, pouncing on, and chasing it, honing their skills so they can hunt with the pride someday.

Lions often snuggle when resting.

Leader of the Pack

Each big cat litter has one cub that emerges as the leader. It's often a bit bigger, a little stronger, or more outgoing than its siblings. With tigers, the dominant cub is often male—and usually gets to be first in line at mealtime.

These almost-grown female tiger cubs play at a water hole in India's Bandhavgarh Tiger Reserve.

Keeping Connected

Lions are very physical: Cubs pull on male lions' manes, rub their cheeks against their mom and aunts, and bite their siblings' tails. It's how they bond. This playful, cuddly contact helps cement the pride's family connection.

Moment of AWWW!!!

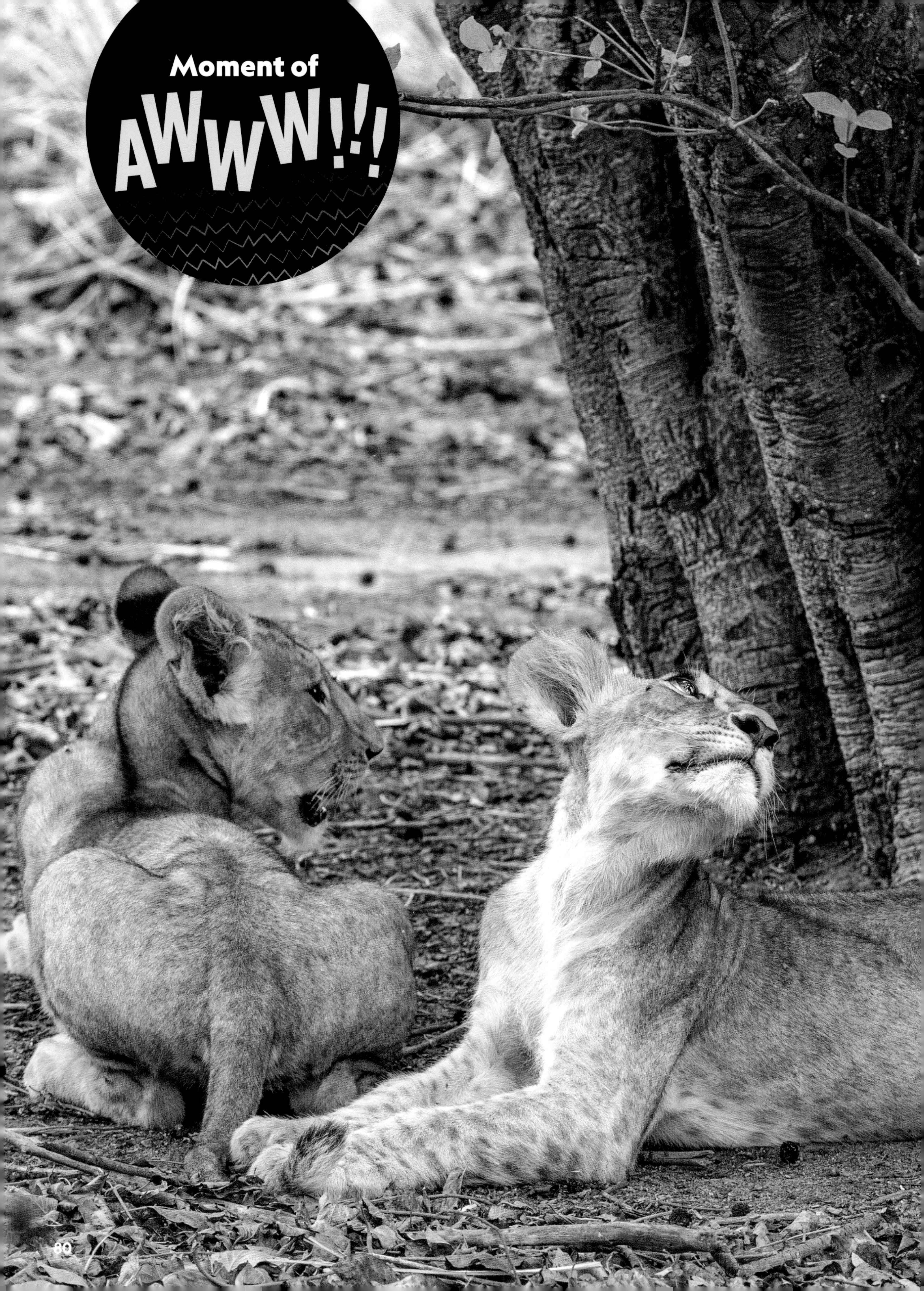

"I am so lucky to work in some of the world's wildest places—and spend weeks or months in the field capturing pictures of animals. I discovered this lion family while photographing in Zakouma National Park in Chad. I was amazed by the connection between these lion cubs and their mother. It didn't seem much different than the bond between a human mom and her kids. They obviously loved each other so much."
—Steve Winter

SAY NO TO ROADSIDE ZOOS

>>> THE THOUGHT OF PETTING BIG CAT CUBS IS TEMPTING, WITH THEIR ADORABLE FACES, FUZZY EARS, AND FUR THAT'S FLUFFIER THAN A PLUSH ANIMAL TOY ON YOUR BED. In the United States, there are roadside zoos that allow visitors to pet and feed cubs. While this may sound like a dream come true, it's dangerous for these animals. For the animals' well-being and your own safety, the only way to spend time with big cats is at a safe distance.

A rescued tiger lounges at a big cat sanctuary.

A BETTER ALTERNATIVE

There are safe ways to see big cats that don't put the cats in harm's way. There are true sanctuaries that save abandoned big cats. These sanctuaries and some larger accredited zoos provide more natural environments for big cats and other wild animals. They don't allow public contact with the animals, and they feed them well and keep them for life.

Tourists bottle-feed a cub in Oklahoma, U.S.A.

Looks Can Be Deceiving

Petting and taking a selfie with a lion cub or feeding a tiger cub a bottle may seem harmless. The cubs are just getting a snack and some cuddles, right? Wrong. There's more to the story. These attractions take newborn cubs away from their mothers as soon as they're born. The babies are often fed formula that's meant for house cat kittens, not big cat cubs, which makes them weak and sick. At between four and eight weeks old, they're put to work and passed around to hundreds of tourists.

Stressful Environment

By four months old, cubs are too big and dangerous to be handled. Then what? Some become breeders, like dogs in a puppy mill. Some are kept on display, often in too-small enclosures and inhumane living conditions with no veterinary care. Owners get rid of the rest because big cats are expensive to keep: It costs about $10,000 a year to feed and provide medical care for an adult tiger. And these roadside zoo cats don't help conservation. Captive-bred tigers are never released into the wild. Because they're used to being around humans, they're a danger to both people and their livestock.

A Growing Problem

The constant breeding needed to supply baby big cats, such as lion and tiger cubs, to these tourist attractions has created what some people call "the U.S. tiger crisis." Although nobody knows exactly how many captive tigers live in the United States, experts think it's more than the 4,000 that remain in the wild in Asia.

Cubs at a lion farm in South Africa

WHEN PREDATORS ARE PREY

Big cat cubs will grow up to be powerful predators, but when they're little, they face threats from all kinds of animals.

>>> BIG CATS CAN KILL THEIR PREY WITH THE BAT OF A PAW. BUT AS CUBS, THEY'RE VULNERABLE, ESPECIALLY WHEN THEIR MOM IS OFF HUNTING. Males of the same species may pose the biggest threat: They see the cubs as intruders. But sometimes the threat is other top predators—or even the prey that these big cats will grow up to eat!

Lion Cubs and Hyenas

Hyenas are fierce carnivores that live in packs. They're mainly scavengers: If there is food to be had, they take it, often feasting on another animal's kill. They are also skilled hunters themselves, and they'll even attack lion cubs. But the food chain travels in both directions—adult lions sometimes prey on hyena cubs, too.

Lions, Hyenas, and Cheetah Cubs

If cheetah cubs are discovered by lions or hyenas, the odds are not in their favor. The first few months of their lives are the riskiest. On Tanzania's Serengeti grasslands, about one in 10 cheetahs survive to adulthood. Attacks from other animals or injuries are the greatest threats. Cheetah mothers can have three, four, or occasionally up to eight cubs. Large litters increase the odds that some of the cubs will survive.

Tiger Cubs and Crocodiles

Tigers, the biggest of the big cats, are at the top of the food chain everywhere they live, so it's hard to imagine them under threat from other predators. But crocodiles, which may live in watering holes or mangrove swamps, occasionally ambush adult tigers or their offspring.

Wolves and Cougar Cubs

When a cougar mom leaves on a hunt, she can be gone for days. To keep her cubs safe, she dens them under fallen trees or in thick brush. But wolves, with their keen sense of smell, sometimes sniff out the hiding spot and attack.

A group of hyenas

Big Cats and Humans

The greatest threat to all big cats isn't other wild animals—it's humans. Poachers hunt big cats for their skins and other parts they sell illegally, often for large sums of money. Farmers and ranchers kill them as revenge for preying on livestock. Some people kill them simply out of fear. If a mother cat dies, her cubs can't fend for themselves unless they're nearly grown up.

Leopards and Lions

One of a leopard cub's greatest threats is from its larger cousin, the lion. But adult leopards have also been known to attack lion cubs.

LIFE AS A LEOPARD CUB

Get Cozy

Before a leopard gives birth, she gives up her nomadic lifestyle and finds a den for her family. Depending on where she lives in Africa or Asia, she must find a cool place to shelter cubs from the desert sun or jungle heat—or find a place to keep them warm in the mountains.

Small Family

Leopard cubs can be born any time of year. The families are usually small, with two or three cubs in a litter.

Early Days

When they enter the world, leopard cubs are blind, their eyes sealed shut. It takes about a week before they get their first look at the world and a month before their first teeth appear.

Close to Home

The helpless infants spend their first eight weeks hidden in a den, surviving on their mother's milk. When mom makes trips out to hunt, she must leave her babies alone. Once they are a few weeks old, she may be gone for up to a day and a half at a time.

Getting Hungry

Leopard cubs grow up quickly. At six weeks, mom brings them their first taste of meat. Soon they will venture out with her. By three months, the cubs are done nursing—and starting to learn the art of hunting their dinner!

A Solo Life

From the time leopards set off to find their own territory, they live a solitary life. They keep to themselves except when mating or raising their young.

Giving Daughters a Home

When their daughters are ready to leave home, mother leopards often give them a piece of their own territory. In fact, related females sometimes cluster together as neighbors: moms, aunts, daughters, and sisters.

WINTER'S TALE

MOM AND CUB

I PHOTOGRAPHED TIGERS ACROSS ASIA FOR A DECADE, BUT IN ALL THAT TIME I'D NEVER GLIMPSED A YOUNG CUB. It was the one part of their lives that I hadn't captured with my camera.

A tiger relies on its mother for two years. What does she teach them? How do they interact? I decided to go to a famous tiger reserve in India to capture images of that special relationship.

When I arrived at Bandhavgarh National Park, a tigress had recently given birth. The man who ran the park's anti-poaching patrol, E. A. Kuttappan, said he would guide me to her den. He and his team tracked the park's tigers and kept an eye out for intruders.

The tigress had birthed her cubs deep in the jungle in exactly the same place where she was born. There were no roads, and it was too dangerous to walk there. You could only get there by elephant.

It was May. Some days hit 120°F (49°C), too hot for an elephant to be saddled and carry us all day. So we had to leave at dawn and head back before noon.

I was perched on a platform seat directly behind Kuttappan, who was the elephant driver. Almost immediately, we were enveloped in nearly impenetrable jungle.

The forest then opened into a narrow gorge that was a sea of brilliant green ferns and moss. We followed a small creek—and then there was mom!

Her den was nestled amid a series of caves, giving her safe places to hide her cubs from predators. And with a creek nearby, she didn't have to leave them for long when she was thirsty.

This tigress had known Kuttappan and his elephant since she was young, so she was relaxed around us. She was about four years old, and this was her first litter.

The tigress was alone—and curious. She moved closer, gliding silently on paws that were the size of dinner plates, then laid down and went to sleep. After an hour, she wandered to the river, drank, and dozed off in a patch of sunlight. The temperature was rising. It was time to go.

This became our daily routine. Most days we'd find her. Sometimes she was probably off hunting. She slept a lot. A few times, we glimpsed tiny stripes—but the cubs were either too small or too timid to reveal themselves. This went on for three weeks.

When we reached the den on the 23rd day, we found mom lying in a beautiful bed of ferns and tangled tree roots. She was up the hill, so I needed to use a long lens that's almost as long as a telescope.

Then I saw a tiny ear behind her. Looking through the viewfinder, I thought I saw a cub emerge and I quickly snapped pictures—but then it was gone. The moment was so quick that I wondered if the cub had come out at all.

Back in camp, I downloaded the memory card. When I saw this picture for the first time, I burst into tears. So much of the tiger story I'd worked on for two years was about poaching, the destruction of the places where tigers live, and conflict with the people who shared their home. But this was hope: an image of the future of the species.

CHAPTER FOUR

HUNT, EAT, SLEEP

>>> A BIG CAT'S SCHEDULE IS PRETTY SIMPLE: HUNT. EAT. PROTECT TURF. SLEEP. REPEAT. But finding prey, successfully capturing it, and making sure other animals don't steal it is hard. And protecting territory can be dangerous!

Because lions hunt in a group and are often out in the open, it's fairly common to see them on safari in Africa. But the other big cats are elusive. Most are rarely seen. This makes it hard for researchers to study where they go and what they do. We're going to take a look at both in-the-field research and some high-tech devices that give scientists—and us!—insight into the secret lives of big cats. Let's peek into their daily routines.

A lioness watches prey move through the grass in Masai Mara National Park, in Kenya.

SOLO ACT

Most big cats live, hunt, and travel by themselves.

>>> **WHILE LIONS ARE SOCIAL ANIMALS, OTHER BIG CATS ARE LONERS.** They only come together to mate or when a mother is raising her young. Two or three male cheetahs or a couple of male lions sometimes team up to hunt and defend their hunting grounds. But for the most part, big cats are out on their own.

An Indochinese tiger stalks through a bamboo forest in Thailand's Huai Kha Khaeng Wildlife Sanctuary.

PROTECTING HOME

There's an important reason why big cats evolved as territorial, solitary creatures: food. These large predators need a lot to eat. Tigers can consume up to 90 pounds (40 kg) of meat in a single meal—that's about the weight of 44 large pizzas. To ensure that other animals don't prey on their prey, tigers establish a home range and guard it carefully. Lions, cheetahs, and leopards also stake out their own domain, even though food is plentiful in their African savanna home. There are many large animals to eat, including wildebeests, zebras, and impalas.

A tiger in India's Bandhavgarh Tiger Reserve stands tall to scratch on a tree.

MARKING TURF

There are telltale signs that you're in big cat territory. Cats leave scent messages for each other, so you may see scrapes scuffed into the dirt or deep scratches etched into trees. Every cat has special glands on its face, between its toes, and at the base of its tail. These glands release pheromones (scented chemicals) whenever cats rub against a bush or scratch something. It's a way for cats to mark their turf or advertise their presence. Since cats ferociously protect their territory, these messages—along with calls— help prevent potentially dangerous encounters with other cats.

A cheetah marks its territory by spraying on a tree trunk in Phinda Game Reserve, in South Africa.

GETTING TERRITORIAL

Cats also spray their musky urine on everything from trees to rocks to tag their turf. But sometimes these sprays are also an invitation for cats to meet during mating season. Scientists think that with their sophisticated sense of smell, cats can learn a lot from these scented messages, including the animal's age, gender, health, and when it left its musky mark.

BIG CAT NAPS

Roaming over a large territory, chasing prey, and dragging it into a hiding place burns a lot of energy. That's why big cats are super snoozers.

Logging Hours

For most children, a typical night's rest is from eight to 12 hours. That's a lot less shut-eye than most big cats get. Lions sleep up to 22 hours a day! Cats have a hunt-feed-rest cycle: They find their prey, chase it down, eat a protein-packed meal, and lie down for a nap. Since lions are at the top of the food chain, they can nap peacefully because they don't have to worry about being eaten while they sleep!

Leopard

Limb Lounging

Leopards are incredible climbers. They spend so much time in trees that they sometimes fall asleep sprawled on a high branch with their paws hanging over the sides.

Daytime Naps

The middle of the day is blisteringly hot in the tropical forests and on the grassy savannas where jaguars, lions, and some leopards and tigers live. So these cats nap in the shade until it cools down. Lions often cuddle with their heads on each other. Females that need to feed hungry cubs—and keep a watchful eye on their busy, playful babies—get less sleep.

Cheetah

Jaguar brothers nap together in Brazil's Pantanal.

SUPER **EXPRESSIVE**

Big cats' facial expressions give clues about how they're feeling. Can you guess each cat's mood?

Lion

Roaring

Sometimes a lion's roar is the cat's way of proclaiming his territory, a kind of warning to other cats to stay away. But this male lion's face is contorted in an angry roar as he squares off with a lioness.

Flehmen behavior

"Flehmen" is a German word that means "lip curl"—which is exactly what cats do when they have a flehmen response. It may look like they're snarling, but they are actually using a special sense to investigate an interesting smell.

Leopard

Relaxed

This tiger gazes at the camera as it cools off in a watering hole during the heat of the day in India. Its sleepy, half-closed eyes show that it is calm.

Tiger

Snarling

This cheetah's curled, open mouth and fully retracted ears indicate that it is feeling defensive, quite possibly because it encountered something unfamiliar and frightening.

Cheetah

Leopard

Yawning/sleeping

When a cat feels safe and falls asleep, its face muscles—and entire body—go completely limp.

BIG BITES

Sekhmet, one of the oldest known Egyptian gods, had a **WOMAN'S BODY AND A LION'S HEAD.**

Jaguars hunt during the day and at night and may travel six miles (10 km) **SEARCHING FOR A MEAL.**

A lion's mane intimidates other males and attracts females, which **PREFER FULL DARK MANES** that may show strength and the ability to fight for the pride.

To protect jaguars in Central America, researchers have set up audio recorders to **LISTEN IN ON POACHERS:** Guards swoop in if they hear loud noises or people talking.

Some snow leopards have **MASSIVE TERRITORIES,** prowling across 386 square miles (1,000 sq km).

In Norse mythology, the goddess Freyja was **ASSOCIATED WITH CATS.** Farmers sought protection for their crops by leaving pans of milk in their fields for the two gray cats that pulled Freya's chariot.

Scientists have discovered that the snow leopard's closest living relative isn't the leopard— **IT'S THE TIGER!**

A group of leopards is called **A LEAP;** a group of tigers is called **A STREAK OR AN AMBUSH.**

Cheetahs generally spend **88 PERCENT OF THEIR DAY RESTING UP** for their next hunt—and they only need to drink once every three or four days.

Scientists at the Massachusetts Institute of Technology designed **A MINI CHEETAH ROBOT** that does far more than the real cat: It can do backflips and walk upside down!

Moment of
AWWW!!!

"Capturing an image of a snow leopard in a snowstorm was incredible luck. Believe it or not, it didn't snow very much during the four months I camped high in India's Himalayan mountains. But I didn't physically shoot this photo. All of my snow leopard pictures were made with remote camera traps that I set up on trails. These elusive cats avoid people: I never saw one up close—though I did glimpse a few in the far distance."

—Steve Winter

HOW TO TRACK A BIG CAT

Most big cats are secretive and don't want to be seen. So when researchers are trying to count big cats or track where they go, they can't just walk into the savanna, forest, mountains, or jungle and easily spot them. Finding big cats often takes detective work—as well as high-tech tools that can unveil the mysteries of their everyday lives.

Wildlife biologist Jeff Sikich searches for signals from a cougar's tracking collar in Southern California, U.S.A.

Say Cheese!

How do you study a cat that you may never even see? Take a picture of it! Scientists and photographers set up camera traps along trails or near water holes, dens, or marking spots—anywhere they know an animal might visit. These are essentially selfie stations! When an animal walks past, it breaks an invisible infrared beam of light and triggers the trap, snapping its own up-close photo. Conservationists count how many individuals appear in these pictures, which allows them to estimate how many cats live in a particular area.

Eyes in the Sky

Snow leopards are among the toughest animals to study. That's because it's nearly impossible for people to follow them in the high, jagged, remote mountains in Asia where they live. But no matter where they call home, all big cats are hard to locate, difficult to safely get close to—or both. So there's only one way to learn more about their natural behaviors and habits and help protect them. Scientists use tranquilizer darts to put a few animals to sleep temporarily so they can fit them with heavy-duty GPS collars. Satellites pick up signals from the collars and researchers download the data on their laptops, allowing them to track the cats' movements every day.

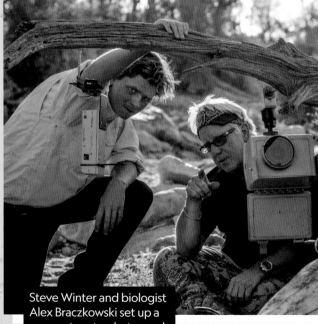

Steve Winter and biologist Alex Braczkowski set up a camera trap to photograph leopards in Sri Lanka.

BEHIND THE SCENES WITH COUGAR SCIENTIST
MARK ELBROCH

Mark Elbroch directs a cougar research program for Panthera, an organization that studies and protects big cats. He's a biologist and an expert tracker who is uncovering the secret behaviors of these elusive cats.

WHY IS IT IMPORTANT FOR SCIENTISTS TO STUDY WILDLIFE?

ELBROCH: There are two reasons: to learn more about wildlife and to help conserve it. Tracking animals helps us count how many are in an area and lets us see trends: Are their numbers going up? Going down? Are they stable?

HOW ARE CAMERA TRAPS USEFUL FOR TRACKING COUGARS?

ELBROCH: Camera traps are fantastic because you don't have to touch the animal. The cameras do all the work! With animals like leopards or tigers, which have identifiable spots and stripes, you can watch and record individual cats.

HOW IMPORTANT ARE GPS COLLARS FOR YOUR WORK?

ELBROCH: You can find lions and cheetahs out in the open. But the other cats are really hard to find without technological aids like GPS collars. When a cat is collared, we know where it is, where it stopped, and how far it traveled. We can ask questions like "Why is it spending time in a certain place?" Then we can go find out. There may be a carcass there, or a den.

National Park Service biologist Jeff Sikich measures a sedated cougar before outfitting it with a satellite collar.

HOW DO YOU PUT A COLLAR ON A BIG CAT?

ELBROCH: First we capture the cat with a snare or a large box trap. Then we use a dart gun to administer an anesthetic that keeps it sedated for about 50 minutes. While monitoring its breathing, heart rate, and temperature, we get to work, taking measurements and weighing it. We take a blood sample for DNA testing and to check for diseases. Then we put the collar on it. The battery will last about two years before we have to replace it. Collaring is the most dangerous thing we do—for us and the animal. It's always a great relief when it's done.

WHAT HAVE GPS COLLARS AND CAMERA TRAPS TAUGHT YOU ABOUT COUGARS?

ELBROCH: We knew that cougars got together once in a while, but we thought it was mostly to mate or fight. But the GPS data, which gives us continuous locations, revealed they were coming together more frequently. A camera trap I set up by a kill showed cougars eating together.

IS THERE NEW TECHNOLOGY ON THE HORIZON FOR ANIMAL TRACKING?

ELBROCH: Yes—lighter-weight collars with longer battery life. Some collars have cameras on them so we can see what the animal sees. Soon we'll have even better video feeds from those.

TOP OF THEIR GAME

Apex predators like big cats play an important role in ecosystems.

>>> BIG CATS SHARE A SPECIAL CATEGORY WITH GREAT WHITE SHARKS, WOLVES, POLAR BEARS, CROCODILES, AND ORCAS: ALL ARE APEX PREDATORS. This means they're at the tip-top of the food chain, rarely vulnerable to other animals except when they're young. Apex predators have an important role: By eating animals that would overpopulate an area and damage the ecosystem, they keep nature in balance. They prey on the weak, the sick, and animals that would take over, including deer, raccoons, coyotes, and others.

Gulf Islands, Canada

The Gulf Islands in Canada show the importance of top predators and what happens when they disappear. About a century ago, cougars, wolves, and other predators were killed off by hunters. Today, raccoons—whose numbers would have been kept in check if these large predators were still around—are devastating songbirds, crabs, and some species of fish.

A cougar cub rests after eating an elk carcass near Jackson Hole, Wyoming, U.S.A.

Zion National Park, U.S.A.

At Utah's Zion National Park, the high number of tourists scared away cougars. The cats' main prey, mule deer, multiplied and devoured many of the cottonwood trees that grow along rivers. This in turn destroyed much of the habitat for lizards, butterflies, fish, and other species, and their numbers dropped. An ecosystem is like a row of carefully placed dominoes: When one link in the food chain is altered, that disturbance ripples through the whole system.

COMPETITION AT THE TOP

What happens when top predators like cougars and wolves cross paths?

>>> BIG CATS HAVE VERY LITTLE TO FEAR—UNTIL ANOTHER APEX PREDATOR STROLLS INTO THEIR NEIGHBORHOOD.

Cougars and wolves compete for food, especially in the American West. But cougars are in the most danger. Packs of wolves chase and attack them—and drive them away from their kills. Biologists watched cougars change their habits after wolves were reintroduced to Yellowstone National Park in Wyoming in 1995. They were shocked to discover that some cougars began to "pride up." Adult males, females, and cubs came together to eat, just like lions do, and mothers adopted other cougars' orphaned cubs. Did they always behave this way? Or have they become more social to defend their food and their young against wolves? Biologist Mark Elbroch and others are trying to find out.

Hide-and-Seek

Cougars now avoid hunting out in the open where wolf packs can easily surround them. They prefer to stalk their prey in forests or rocky areas where they can hide or escape from wolves.

Once they catch and kill an animal, they feed on it for up to five days. Cougars (and other big cats) cache the carcasses between meals, concealing them under leaves, branches, or dirt. But sometimes hiding their prey doesn't help: Wolves, bears, or other predators may sniff out a cougar's kill and steal it.

APEX PECKING ORDER

Grizzly bear

Jaguar

Cougar

Gray wolf

One study revealed that cougars are top predators in almost half their range. They dominate coyotes and South America's maned wolves. But when they coexist with wolves, grizzly bears, black bears, or jaguars, they take a step down on the predator ladder. In this illustration, bold arrows point from the apex predator to its prey. Thin arrows indicate when prey becomes a predator, too.

Coyote

Maned wolf

American black bear

WHAT'S ON THE MENU

Elk is a cougar's favorite food, but this cat is not a picky eater. A study of 473 cougar kills between 1998 and 2005 in Yellowstone National Park showed that they ate everything from deer and bighorn sheep to eagles and porcupines.

Elk
76%

Other
3%

Marmots
2%

Pronghorn
2%

Bighorn sheep
3%

Mule deer
14%

ON THE HUNT

Each big cat species has its own hunting style.

Tigers

A tiger's black stripes act as an invisibility cloak, helping it blend into the landscape as it hunts in the dim light of dusk, dawn, or under cover of darkness. This cat stalks silently to within yards of its unsuspecting target, and then chases and pounces with stunning force. Tigers can bring down animals three times their weight with their sharp claws and massive paws that are nearly as big as dinner plates! But even they must be careful: Their prey's thrashing hooves or horns could be deadly.

A tiger feeds on a sambar deer.

Lions

Lions are fantastic hunters, but if they wander across a leopard's or cheetah's hard-won dinner, they take over to scavenge a free meal.

Cheetahs

Unlike other big cats, cheetahs usually hunt during the day, so they don't even attempt to hide on the flat African savanna. Cheetahs walk toward a herd until the animals flee, and then they sprint after one individual. They can turn in midair to follow their zigzagging victim, and they often swat at its back legs to trip it. The chase is over in 20 to 60 seconds. Then cheetahs must gulp their meal or drag the animal to a safe spot. Since they're at the bottom of the predator chain, cheetahs often lose their kill to lions, leopards, jackals, or hyenas.

Leopards

Leopards usually hunt on the ground, ambushing prey with an explosive charge at close range. But in Africa's Serengeti National Park, they're known to attack from above—by leaping from trees! Like most big cats, they clamp on to their victim's throat for a quick kill.

HUNTING SUCCESS RATES

Big cats may be strong and mighty hunters, but that doesn't mean they always succeed on the first pounce. Prey often gets away. Most attempts end in failure. Here's how big cats' hunting skills measure up to those of other carnivores.

Animal	Success Rate
TIGERS	5%
POLAR BEARS	10%
WOLVES	14%
LIONS	25%
DOMESTIC CATS	32%
LEOPARDS	38%
CHEETAHS	50%
AFRICAN WILD DOGS	85%
DRAGONFLIES	95%

Tiger · Polar bear · Wolf · Lion · Domestic cat · Leopard · Cheetah · African wild dog · Dragonflies

0% 25% 50% 75% 100%

EXTRAORDINARY HUNTERS

Big cats' bodies, senses, and skills are perfectly evolved to survive as carnivores, or meat-eaters.

Night Vision

Most big cats are crepuscular, hunting mostly during the low-light hours of dawn or twilight, and sometimes at night. They can see in the dark. Cats' big eyes are lined with special cells that act like a mirror. These cells reflect light, giving cats spectacular night vision, and this makes their eyes seem to shine in the dark. In dim light, jaguars can see about six times better than people.

A jaguar hunting for prey at dusk hides in tall grass in Brazil's Pantanal wetlands.

Tiger

Ears, Whiskers, and Paws

With their extraordinary hearing, tigers can detect prey a mile (1.6 km) away. Special hairs inside a jaguar's ears act like antennae, picking up distant sounds. All cats use their long whiskers to navigate in the dark. They can also sense vibrations from another animal's movement through touch-sensitive hairs on their paws.

Group Dynamics

Teamwork is the best hunting strategy for lions living on the wide-open savanna where they're easily spotted. The females are the main hunters. Often, one group charges a herd of animals, stampeding them into a trap where other lions await. Together, they can take down huge animals, from wildebeests to giraffes. The strongest males and females usually eat first. Fights break out when food is scarce. Weaker adults and cubs eat last and may go hungry. When lone males hunt, they ambush from shrubby vegetation. It's hard to hide in open grasslands with a big mane.

Sharp Claws, Specialized Teeth, and a Scratchy Tongue

Big cats (except for cheetahs) use their razor-sharp claws and huge canine teeth to grab an animal so they can deliver a fatal bite. Other teeth act like knives to slice off meat, and sharp bristles on their tongues, called papillae, scrape the bones clean.

Researchers inspect a tranquilized jaguar's teeth to determine its age and health.

Working together, lions can hunt large animals.

WHAT'S FOR **DINNER?**

Most big cats hunt and scavenge many kinds of animals. But when food is in short supply, they will catch nearly anything—and sometimes resort to killing cattle, sheep, yaks, and other domestic animals. Here's a list of the prey each cat prefers.

Lion

- African buffalo
- Blue wildebeest
- Cheetah cubs
- Giraffe
- Impala
- Spotted hyena
- Thomson's gazelle
- Young elephant
- Young rhino
- Zebra

Tiger

- Chital
- Gray langur monkeys
- Guar
- Sambar deer
- Water buffalo
- Wild pigs

Snow leopard

- Asiatic ibex
- Himalayan blue sheep
- Himalayan tahr
- Markhor
- Marmot
- Pika

Leopard

Antelope
Barbary wild boar
Blue wildebeest
Deer
Fish

Gazelle
Monkeys
Rodents

Jaguar

Caiman
Capybara
Deer
Fish
Peccary
Snakes
Tapir
Turtles

Cougar

Deer
Gazelle
Mice

Porcupine
Rabbit
Raccoon

Cheetah

Greater kudu
Hare
Impala
Ostrich
Springbok

Thomson's gazelle
Wildebeest calves

LEAST PICKY EATER AWARD:
THE JAGUAR

Jaguars are great climbers and excellent swimmers, and they eat almost anything they can catch in the water or on land. Their main food is capybaras (a rodent that weighs 75 to 145 pounds [35 to 66 kg]) and peccaries (wild pigs). And in Brazil, they regularly leap off steep banks into rivers to capture caimans, fighting them above and below the water's surface. But jaguars feast on more than 80 species, from iguanas, snakes, and monkeys to armadillos and sloths. They've even been observed dipping their tails in rivers to lure fish! Jaguars are the only cats that kill with a deadly bite to the back of the skull, and they can pierce a turtle's hard shell with their powerful jaws.

WINTER'S TALE

IN THE LAND OF LEOPARDS

DURING TWO YEARS OF PHOTO-GRAPHING LEOPARDS, I LEARNED THAT THEY'RE REALLY ADAPTABLE. They stalk steamy jungles; survive harsh, freezing winters in Siberia; and endure sizzling summers across Africa and Asia. They live in mountains, grasslands, deserts, and in a mega-city in India—and they spend nearly as much time in the trees as they do on the ground.

One of the places I photographed them was a leopard haven. Sabi Sands is a private game reserve adjoining a national park in South Africa. These usually shy cats are so used to seeing tourists watching them from safari vehicles that they're not afraid of people. That made my job a lot easier.

My guide knew these cats and was great at finding them. He gave me safety instructions, as curious cats occasionally sauntered right next to our open Jeep, which was both thrill-ing and scary. But they usually ignored us. Sometimes I spent hours with a leopard that was resting during the heat of the day—or with a family, watching cubs playing, sleeping, or rolling around with their mom. If they were disturbed by our presence, we didn't chase them. Respect for these animals is my top priority. It's their home, not mine.

To find them, my guide reminded me to look up in the trees. These climbing cats are unique: Leopards lounge on limbs, catching a breeze, relaxing in safety off the ground, or eating. Their spotted coats camouflaged them amid the leaves, and I often didn't see a cat until someone pointed it out.

Near dusk one day, someone radioed on the walkie-talkie, sending us to a tree where this cat was sleeping. It eventually walked over to an antelope that it had left draped over a branch and leisurely ate its meal. Tree-dining is the only way leopards can protect their kill—and themselves—from lions, hyenas, or other predators.

But climbing a tree won't protect them from people, and part of my job is to document the threats that wildlife face. Farmers and ranchers hunt leopards and poach them for their skins.

In South Africa, leopard skins are used in Nazareth Baptist Church cere-monies. This faith was founded a cen-tury ago, blending Zulu customs and Christian beliefs. I was the first outsider allowed to witness and photograph their festivals. Every Sunday in July, tens of thousands gather on a sacred hill, the men dressed in traditional Zulu warrior regalia—draped in leopard skin capes.

Zoologist Tristan Dickerson was study-ing leopards in South Africa when police raided a nearby village and discovered 92 leopard skins. He realized that these ceremonies were taking a serious toll. So he brainstormed a solution that saves leopards' lives and also preserves cultural traditions: faux fur capes. He searched for the best-looking fake fur he could find, and church leaders agreed to use them. He has now given away thousands of capes, and he hopes that soon all participants will choose them over the real thing. His success is inspiring: Great new ideas can save wildlife!

In Sri Lanka's Yala National Park, leopards wander out of the forest and onto the beach to hunt at night.

CHAPTER FIVE

IN **CAT** TERRITORY

» **BIG CATS ARE AT HOME IN ALL KINDS OF PLACES, FROM SNOWY MOUNTAIN PEAKS TO STEAMY JUNGLES.** And these felines are flexible with their hangout spots, too: Depending on their species, they can be found lounging on a tree limb, lying in the grass, or soaking in a swampy lagoon. They wander along beaches, while water-loving tigers and jaguars swim wide rivers.

Big cats have had to adapt to a wide range of habitats in order to survive, largely because the number of humans on the planet—now almost eight billion— has doubled in the last 50 years. That's left these cats with only fragmented scraps of habitat. But even though humans are the source of the problem, they've also become part of the solution. People around the world are working to secure space for cats to live and thrive. Let's tour big cat territory, and also look at some creative solutions to save their homelands.

MAKING A
SPLASH

Jaguars and tigers are agile swimmers that regularly take a plunge.

DINING **SPOT**

Since all animals need water to survive, watering holes are gathering places. For big cats, they're also hunting grounds, great places to stalk animals that have paused for a drink. Jaguars that live in Brazil's Pantanal wetlands dive right into rivers to grab caimans bigger than they are, and sometimes almost drown before subduing these reptiles.

A jaguar leaps into the Cuiabá River in Brazil in pursuit of a caiman.

GOING THE DISTANCE

Both tigers and jaguars love the water, and they're powerful swimmers. Jaguars have been spotted paddling across the Panama Canal, a distance equivalent to about six lengths of an Olympic-size pool. Tigers also swim long distances, crossing rivers or swimming between islands in the salty Bay of Bengal's mangrove swamps.

A tiger crosses a salty inlet in India's Sundarbans mangroves in the Bay of Bengal.

A FELINE THAT FISHES FOR FOOD

Some smaller cats like water, too, including the stocky, medium-size fishing cat. This nocturnal feline thrives in the marshy, boggy wetlands of South and Southeast Asia. The fishing cat dives deep to catch crabs and frogs with its teeth. Sometimes it stays in shallow water to grab fish, its favorite food, with its paws. The webbing between its toes helps it swim fast, scoop up fish, and walk on muddy shorelines. To keep warm and dry, this cat has two layers of fur, much like water dogs do, that repel water and insulate against the cold.

Fishing cat

UP A TREE

Most big cats spend their time on the ground—that's where most of their food is. But leopards and jaguars, and occasionally lions, also spend time in trees. Here's why.

A Bird's-Eye View

Trees can serve as an observation tower or a hunting platform for leopards, jaguars, and cheetahs. A high branch offers a strategic vantage point for spotting and ambushing prey.

Climbing a tree gives this cheetah a hunting advantage: a view of the entire landscape.

Two leopards cool off—and watch over their territory.

Cool and Breezy

The rainforests and savannas where many big cats live are brutally hot. Some big cats climb up onto leafy branches to rest in the shade and catch a little breeze.

Safe Space

Leopards are incredible climbers, and they're strong. They can drag prey three times heavier than they are up into a tree! High in the branches, they can safely eat their hard-won meal without losing it to scavengers such as hyenas, wild dogs, or lions.

A leopard in South Africa enjoys its meal from on high.

TREE-CLIMBING LIONS

The lion prides in Uganda's Queen Elizabeth National Park are extremely unique: They spend part of their lives in the wide branches of fig and acacia trees. Cat biologist Alex Braczkowski lived there for a year to study these special lions. He believes that they climb up to escape the heat, survey the landscape, and escape constant, painful bites from the tsetse flies that infest these grasslands.

BIG BITES

Ancient Egyptians thought giraffes were a
HYBRID OF A CAMEL AND A LEOPARD.

Cats may have the
LARGEST EYES
for their body size of any mammal.

Unlike other mammals, cats
CANNOT TASTE SWEETNESS.

A big cat's tongue is
COVERED WITH TINY RASPS,
or hooks, that are so sharp
they can draw blood
just by licking.

Tigers were so revered in Korea that for many centuries military officials wore **BADGES WITH TIGERS EMBROIDERED** on them to signify their strength and courage.

Some Siberian tigers live at the **TOP OF THE WORLD,** north of the Arctic Circle.

Researchers at New York City's Bronx Zoo discovered that **MEN'S COLOGNE MAKES BIG CATS GO CRAZY:** When they smell it, they rub against things, drool, and go into a trancelike state.

A caracal can **SWAT A BIRD FROM THE SKY** with a single paw.

According to African legend, the black marks on a cheetah's face **ARE TEAR STAINS,** and the cat is crying because it can't figure out if it's a dog or a cat.

Relatives of the **CARACAL WERE THE FIRST CATS IN AFRICA.** They walked across a land bridge from Asia eight to 10 million years ago.

SHRINKING HOMELAND

With nearly eight billion people on Earth, there's much less room for wildlife. Here are the ways that our growing population has impacted big cat habitat.

Forests Down

Much of what was big cat territory is now farmland, towns, cities, roads, factories, and stores. This leaves wildlife with little area to live in, and big cats need big territories. With forests gone, cats have less prey to hunt, and they come into closer contact with humans, which is dangerous for both cats and people.

Plantations (left) are replacing the thick rainforest (right) in Sumatra that is home to tigers and many other species.

Heavy Traffic

Roads, highways, and railroads now crisscross big cat territory. Crossing busy roadways is dangerous. In some places, like India's Kaziranga Tiger Reserve, highways even cut through national parks, which are prime big cat habitat. Roads also give poachers easier access to animals.

Many animals die attempting to cross roads; safely navigating a highway is nearly impossible.

Urban Sprawl

Even though big cats are wild, sometimes they are forced into city life. Because of urban sprawl—the expansion of cities and towns on undeveloped land—the boundary between a big cat's territory and human communities is sometimes very close and may even overlap.

A bobcat stands on a hill overlooking the Golden Gate Bridge, in San Francisco, California, U.S.A.

When forests are leveled, animals lose both their homes and food sources.

Palm Oil

Sumatran tigers are critically endangered. Perhaps 400 remain, and they don't have much land left to live on. Much of their lush rainforest home on the Indonesian island of Sumatra is gone, cut down to produce palm oil. This oil is used in almost half of the packaged products we find in grocery stores—from pizza, doughnuts, and chocolate to deodorant, shampoo, toothpaste, and lipstick. But palm oil isn't the only problem. Big cat habitat is also cut down to grow cotton, coffee, and many other products, and to raise cattle sold for meat.

SAFE PASSAGE

Bridges and tunnels can help wildlife cross busy roads.

A wildlife overpass spans the Trans-Canada Highway in Banff, Alberta, Canada.

>>> **WHY DID THE COUGAR CROSS THE ROAD? BECAUSE THERE WAS A BRIDGE TO WALK OVER!**

Roads are danger zones for all wildlife, including big cats. And they're a huge threat: Google Earth images show that roads are nearly everywhere except protected lands. The United States alone has some four million miles (6.4 million km) of roads, the equivalent of almost 17 trips to the moon! Cars and trucks kill between one and two million large animals every year on U.S. roads. Conservationists are creating safe passages for four-legged foot traffic in some places by convincing state officials to build tunnels, underpasses and overpasses, culverts, and barriers.

ANIMAL-FRIENDLY

To entice wildlife across bridges and through tunnels, these passages are covered in native plants so that they blend into the landscape. Tunnels, or underpasses, go underneath highways to help both large and small animals travel from one side to the other. It can take a few years for some animals, like cougars, bears, and elk, to feel comfortable using bridges. But in time, the generations all fall in step, as mothers lead cubs across overpasses and they become part of the cats' normal routes.

Overpasses covered in vegetation, like this one, blend into an animal's natural environment and can help them cross busy roads safely.

SPREADING OUT

Big cats need to cover a lot of ground to find food and mates. When they can safely cross roads, cats can expand their range into essential habitats. They can also mingle with a greater number of animals, which reduces inbreeding among a smaller population. That's a good thing, as the offspring of close relatives may have serious health problems.

CULVERTS FOR CATS

A panther uses a newly added ledge to cross under a road in LaBelle, Florida, U.S.A.

Speeding vehicles are particularly deadly for Florida panthers that live in a densely populated U.S. state crisscrossed by roads. Collisions are the leading cause of death for this critically endangered cougar subspecies. The Florida Department of Transportation has built 60 wildlife bridges and underpasses, from small cement culverts under roadways to tunnels. Long fences guide the animals to these safe crossings.

BIG CATS IN THE BIG CITY

In Mumbai, India, a megacity of almost 20 million people, more than 40 leopards live right in the middle of the city, in and around Sanjay Gandhi National Park.

A Populated Park

These leopards may be city dwellers, surrounded by buildings, people, and bright lights, but Sanjay Gandhi National Park is a haven. It's 40 square miles (104 sq km)—30 times the size of New York City's Central Park. That's still tight quarters for a cat that can wander 18 miles (29 km) a day. There are more cats living there than you'd find in a same-size area in the best leopard territory in Africa.

Food Options

Mumbai's leopards thrive on spotted deer, wild boar, and other favored prey in the park. But at night, some cats wander through city streets and alleys to catch urban animal residents, including pigs, rats, chickens, goats, and stray dogs.

Human Interactions

Leopards lived in Mumbai long before it bustled with millions of people. Now with legal and illegal settlements inside the park, people and cats are side by side—and living with predators is dangerous. It's rare, but leopards sometimes kill people. The city had up to 30 attacks each year until the Indian government started education programs that teach residents what to do if they encounter a leopard: Don't panic, make noise, or disturb it—just let it pass. Rescue teams swoop in to tranquilize and remove problem leopards. Now there are fewer attacks, and many people are more accepting of leopards as their neighbors.

Leopards drink from a well in Mumbai.

Cats and Dogs

Packs of dogs roam loose in Mumbai, about 95,000 dogs in all. Some of these strays have rabies, and they bite about 750,000 people each year. But leopards hunt and kill the dogs, which make up almost half of their diet. In the process, the cats are protecting their human neighbors. Villagers who live near the national park are 90 percent less likely to be bitten by a dog than those who live farther away.

Moment of AHHH!?!

"I always learn surprising things when I work with scientists on stories. Finding out that leopards live in a national park in Mumbai, India—one of the world's largest cities—was one of those moments. It took a few weeks to capture this image on a camera trap. When I showed it to some of the people who lived in this building, they were shocked: Some didn't even know they had leopards for neighbors, and most had never seen one!"

—Steve Winter

THE JAGUAR FREEWAY

Biologists once believed there were eight subspecies of jaguar. But in 2001, DNA studies proved that it's actually the same cat throughout its range, from Mexico's deserts to the grasslands of northern Argentina. This means that these cats wander millions of square miles through 18 countries to breed.

>>> BUT NOW, BECAUSE OF RAMPANT DEVELOPMENT, THEY LIVE IN SCRAPS OF FOREST AND ISOLATED RESERVES THAT ARE CUT OFF FROM EACH OTHER. Biologist Alan Rabinowitz worried that if jaguars remained cut off, they would become inbred and unhealthy. So he conceived a unique conservation strategy, one that had never been attempted before.

Creating Connection

The Jaguar Corridor Initiative is now creating routes for jaguars to move safely between their strongholds. Rabinowitz and his team identified 182 pathways where the cats' habitat could be connected, all the way through Central and South America. This network would link up 90 separate jaguar populations.

To "build" this corridor, biologists with the conservation group Panthera are collaborating with governments and private landowners. As long as there's some water and places to hide, jaguars can move through any landscape, including ranches, farms, and plantations. They travel mostly at night.

A jaguar slips through a cattle fence in Brazil.

This male jaguar swam across the Cuiabá River in Brazil right after this photo was taken.

A herd of water buffalo in the Brazilian Pantanal

More Solutions

A big challenge has been educating ranchers. In Brazil's Pantanal wetlands, any time a cow died, ranchers blamed jaguars, so they hunted the cats. Then biologist Sandra Cavalcanti put GPS collars on jaguars. By tracking their movements, she proved that they rarely killed cattle and helped convince ranchers not to shoot them.

Panthera pioneered new protections for cattle, adding water buffalo to herds. The buffalo encircle calves and battle intruders, while cows stampede, leaving slower calves at risk. And corralling pregnant females and calves at night within electric fences discourage even the hungriest cat!

WINTER'S TALE

A COUGAR CELEBRITY

IN SOUTHERN CALIFORNIA, COUGARS LIVE ON SCRAPS OF LAND IN AN AREA POPULATED BY HUMANS AND CUT UP BY ROADWAYS. The 10-lane 101 Freeway, one of the busiest roads in the United States, separates the two largest protected areas. It's almost impossible for animals to cross safely. These cougars face local extinction.

I scouted the area with wildlife biologist Jeff Sikich, who studied cougars for the National Park Service. He outfitted the cats with satellite collars that beamed their locations to his laptop. With maps of their movements, he could help me figure out where to set up my camera traps.

I needed to show that these cats were urban dwellers. I joked with Jeff, "Wouldn't it be great to get a picture of a cougar under the Hollywood sign?" He thought I was crazy. No cats lived there.

Jeff called me a few months later. "You're not going to believe this!" he said. A male cougar was in downtown Los Angeles! Somehow he'd made it across two freeways alive and moved into Griffith Park, where the Hollywood sign is. He was probably seeking his own territory, as "teenage" cougars must. Jeff named him P-22, short for Puma 22. (Puma is one of many names for cougars.) He tranquilized him and put on a tracking collar.

Setting up expensive cameras in a city park is complicated. Ten million people visit Griffith Park each year. And we couldn't predict whether P-22 would come by—or when.

I captured pictures of raccoons, people walking their dogs, runners, deer, a bobcat. But all of my cameras, secured in heavy, locked steel cases, were eventually stolen—except for one on a trail only used by animals. But it was the lucky one. After 14 months, P-22 finally walked by and snapped this photo of himself. It was better than what I'd envisioned—and it was a reminder to dream big and never give up!

This picture appeared in newspapers, magazines, films, and on TV. P-22 became an ambassador for urban wildlife, with his own exhibit at the Natural History Museum of Los Angeles County. October 24 was declared P-22 Day in Los Angeles. City schools now study urban wildlife in their science programs. P-22 is how people think about wildlife and the ways we can coexist with animals.

Beth Pratt, who directs the National Wildlife Federation's California program, made a life-size print of P-22, cut it out, and carried it around the state for years. This big cat celebrity "met" thousands of people, including the governor, lawmakers, movie stars, and schoolkids, as Beth advocated for construction of a wildlife overpass for the 101 Freeway. It would connect two protected areas, offering the best chance for the cougar's survival. And since big cats are wide-ranging predators, protecting them also protects every other animal that shares their homeland.

P-22 was still living in Griffith Park when we wrote this book. The overpass was scheduled to break ground in early 2022. It is California's first wildlife overpass—and will be the largest one in the world.

CHAPTER SIX

ANCIENT CATS

>>> CAN YOU IMAGINE WHAT IT WOULD BE LIKE TO SEE AN ENORMOUS CAT PROWLING THROUGH GRASSLANDS—ONE WITH DAGGERLIKE TEETH THAT WERE SO BIG THEY PROTRUDED OUT OF ITS MOUTH AND REACHED PAST ITS LOWER JAW? Or can you envision domestic cats in ancient Egypt being waited on and treated like royalty? Jaguars worshipped as gods in Latin America? It might sound like fiction, but catlike species have been around for millions of years and have a wild-but-true history with humans.

A mythical creature with a human head and a lion's body, ancient Egypt's Great Sphinx stands among the pyramids in Giza, Egypt.

PREHISTORIC CATS

Long before today's big cats appeared, ancient catlike carnivores roamed the planet.

>>> THE MOST ANCIENT BIG CAT ANCESTOR WAS ABOUT THE SIZE OF YOUR PET CAT, LOOKED A BIT LIKE A MONGOOSE, AND LIVED MORE THAN 30 MILLION YEARS AGO. ITS NAME, *PROAILURUS*, MEANS "FIRST CAT." About 10 million years later, cats evolved into larger species and their family tree split in two. One branch (Felidae) became today's cats, while the other (Machairodontinae) became saber-toothed cats. Early humans lived alongside some of them. They drew images of formidable felines, which still exist preserved in deep caves.

Woolly mammoth and Smilodon cats

A SWORD-TOOTHED CAT

One of the best known saber-toothed cats, *Smilodon fatalis*, was truly a fearsome-looking animal. It was muscular, as big as a grizzly bear, weighed up to 600 pounds (272 kg), and flashed canine fangs that were as long as a carving knife! *Smilodon* lived in what is now North America and South America. They died out about 10,000 years ago, 65 million years after the dinosaurs went extinct. Murals in natural history museums show the cat taking down bison and horses. But fossils unearthed by paleontologists at the La Brea Tar Pits outside Los Angeles, California, U.S.A., revealed that *Smilodon* hunted smaller animals, like deer. These pits—natural asphalt that bubbled up from underground—trapped and preserved thousands of animals, providing a treasure trove of scientific information about that ancient ecosystem.

Smilodon fatalis

American lion skull

THE AMERICAN LION WASN'T A LION

Some 13,000 years ago, a giant big cat that weighed as much as two refrigerators ranged from what is now Alaska southward to Peru. When it was first described in 1853 from a jawbone fossil, the American lion was named *Felis atrox*, or "cruel cat." It's called a lion, but its name is a mistake. After comparing this now extinct cat's skull with those of today's big cats, scientists think it was actually a type of giant jaguar.

AN ANCIENT ANCESTOR COMES TO AMERICA

The Pleistocene jaguar is one of the few ancient cats that still has a living relative. This cat first appeared in Asia about three million years ago and later crossed the Bering Land Bridge. It settled across the Americas, living beside massive "mega-fauna" like mastodons and ground sloths. With a warming climate, floods, and drought during the Pleistocene epoch, these megafauna died off and went extinct. But the prehistoric jaguar survived and evolved into today's slightly smaller jaguar. Ice Age cougars also survived, and scientists think these cats' adaptable eating habits saved them. They seem to have eaten anything, gnawing on bones and thick-skinned prey as well as small animals that other predators ignored.

When three cave explorers ventured deep into a hidden cave in southern France in 1994, they found the bones of extinct cave bears—and some of the world's oldest drawings. Images of animals covered the walls of Chauvet Cave, created by hunter-gatherer Paleolithic people some 30,000 years ago. In a 12-foot (3.7-m) panel, bison seem to race across the rock, fleeing 16 lions. The artwork offers a glimpse into the relationship between humans and big cats. The lions, as symbols of power, were drawn with special attention.

CAVE CATS

TIGER TALES

As symbols of strength and courage, tigers are woven into Asian culture, religion, folklore, and ritual.

>>> IT'S NO WONDER THAT HUMANS HAVE ADMIRED, FEARED, AND REVERED TIGERS FOR THOUSANDS OF YEARS. They're majestic, fierce, and beautiful. They radiate power. They inspire awe. Tigers' stealthy, ghostlike habits—suddenly appearing and disappearing in dense forests, often at night—raised them to the status of otherworldly beings across their entire Asian range.

Tiger painting from China

The four stripes on a tiger's forehead form the **CHINESE CHARACTER WÁNG, WHICH MEANS "KING."**

Otherworldly Powers

In ancient legends across Asia, tigers brought food to men and women lost in the forest. They fought the forces of evil, protecting tribes and villages. They grew wings, flying great distances to cure and heal. They turned white, becoming stars that were part of the Milky Way. Few people dared to kill them, as many tribes believed that tigers carried the spirits of their ancestors.

Tiger Brothers

In a creation story, the Indigenous Naga people living in Myanmar and India believed that the world's first human—a woman—gave birth to the first spirit, the first tiger, and the first man at the same time. That makes humans and tigers family.

This Naga village leader in India wears a tiger-tooth necklace.

Guardians and Gods

Indian mythology teems with tigers. These cats are considered superior beings, worshipped to this day. The Hindu goddess Durga defeated a monster-demon while riding her ferocious mount, a tiger. The tiger god Vaghadeva is the guardian of the forest. Dancers still dress up as tigers or paint their bodies to look like tigers during India's yearly Pulikali festival.

Children in India dressed up as tigers

"The Master"

The forest-dwelling Moi people in Indochina so revered this cat that they called it a host of names that reflected its distinguished reputation: "lofty one," "his eminence," "the master," "my lord," or "the gentlemen"— but never simply "tiger."

Shape-Shifter

In fables from Siberia, China, and other parts of Asia, humans morph into tigers. First, their feet become enormous paws. Their chest and back expand, rippling with muscle, and striped fur covers their skin. A tail appears, and finally, an enormous tiger head emerges. Back in human form, these shape-shifters were said to look normal, except they lacked a groove in their upper lip.

LEGENDARY LIONS

The Greeks feared lions so much that these big cats became the inspiration for many mighty mythical beasts.

>>> **TODAY, LIONS ARE FOUND ONLY IN AFRICA AND IN ONE NATIONAL PARK IN INDIA.** But when the ancient Greeks wrote their legends thousands of years ago, Asiatic lions roamed from southeast Europe across the Middle East to Asia. Lions loomed large in their stories: Their god of fear, Phobos, had a mane, and Heracles, clad in a lion skin, is the strongest mortal and greatest hero in Greek mythology.

People born under the astrological sign Leo (July 23–August 22) **ARE SAID TO BE NATURAL LEADERS,** fearless and strong.

Heracles and the Nemean Lion

In Greek myth, Heracles, the son of the Greek god Zeus, had to complete 12 nearly impossible tasks to become immortal. He had to outsmart or conquer gods and monsters, and his first task was to slay the Nemean lion. This terrifying man-eater was killing local people. Its horrible claws could cut through armor, and it had an impenetrable golden skin that rendered human weapons useless. Heracles trapped the lion in its den and eventually defeated it with his bare hands. He used the hide to make an indestructible cape to protect himself. The lion then rose into the sky and formed the constellation Leo.

The Mighty Griffin

Sometimes its beak is open and its face has a menacing look. The mythological griffin has an eagle's head, wings, and sharp talons—and a lion's powerful body. It pulled the chariot of Apollo (the sun god) between Earth and the sun, and it fiercely guarded gold and other treasures. Since griffins were mighty, wise, and wily, their image was emblazoned on war flags and coats of armor to show military strength. Another hybrid, the sphinx, also has a lion's body, wings, and a woman's head.

The Fire-Breathing Chimera

The female fire-breathing Chimera was another hybrid beast from Greek mythology. It was a kind of Frankenstein's monster: a lion with a goat's head coming out of its back and a serpent's head on the tip of its tail. The Chimera ransacked and destroyed villages. A glimpse of her was considered a bad omen, as she was believed to appear before natural disasters, particularly volcanic eruptions. She was ultimately killed by a hero, Bellerophon, who flew on the winged horse Pegasus.

BIG CATS IN ANCIENT ROME

Because of their strength and power, big cats were legendary, but in ancient Rome, these mighty cats were used in a brutal form of entertainment. Fighting and hunting captive lions and tigers was a big sport. Spectators filled the massive Colosseum to watch face-offs between tigers and lions or between cats and other animals, or fights staged between sword-wielding men and big cats. Emperor Nero celebrated the arena's opening with a "hunt" inside the Colosseum that killed 300 lions.

"Trying to find a cougar in Wyoming's Teton mountains is like looking for a needle in a haystack! Scientists told us about a mom and cub that had been seen nearby. We scoured the area and discovered a cave that was the perfect place for a family to curl up and stay warm. The cub, who we nicknamed Lucky, was about three months old in this photo."

—Steve Winter

Moment of

AWWW!!!

DIVINE FELINES OF THE AMERICAS

The jaguar was never just a big cat—it was a god, revered by peoples across the Americas.

>>> SINCE THE EARLIEST RECORDED HISTORY OF MESOAMERICA (NOW MEXICO AND CENTRAL AMERICA), many peoples believed the fierce, powerful, and secretive jaguar from the dark and dense rainforest had supernatural powers. Rulers or shamans could morph into jaguars—and jaguars could transform into humans.

THE OLMEC
(circa 1500–400 B.C.)

Jaguars have been woven into art, culture, and religion at least as far back as the Olmec civilization in 1150 B.C. The Olmecs even altered the shape of their skulls to resemble jaguars. In their artwork, their fierce deity was depicted as a "were-jaguar": half human, half jaguar.

An Olmec sculpture in the form of a jaguar spirit

THE MAYA
(circa 1500 B.C.– A.D. 1500)

The Maya worshipped jaguars. They had many jaguar gods, including God L, one of the rulers of the Underworld, a supernatural world of the dead. The Maya thought that because jaguars have extraordinary night vision, they could travel between the worlds of the living and the dead. The Maya word for jaguar—*balam*—also means priest or sorcerer.

The Maya built temples to the jaguar. They were places of power, adorned with paintings and carvings of the cat. Warrior kings dressed in jaguar skins and sat on thrones carved in the shape of a jaguar in the ancient cities of Chichen Itza, Palenque, and Uxmal (which today are in Mexico). Archaeologists working in Belize discovered that Maya kings were buried with the animal's skin, claws, and fangs.

The Maya hero Xbalanque (which means Jaguar Sun) harnessed the power of the jaguar. He wore patches of jaguar fur on his body when he defeated the evil Lords of Xibalba, who were believed to rule the Underworld.

The Maya Temple of the Jaguar in Chichen Itza, Mexico

THE AZTEC
(14th–16th century A.D.)

The Aztec also revered the jaguar. They were a warrior culture, and the bravest men were recruited into the distinguished Jaguar Knights, who wore jaguar skins and masks in combat.

An Aztec stone sculpture of a jaguar

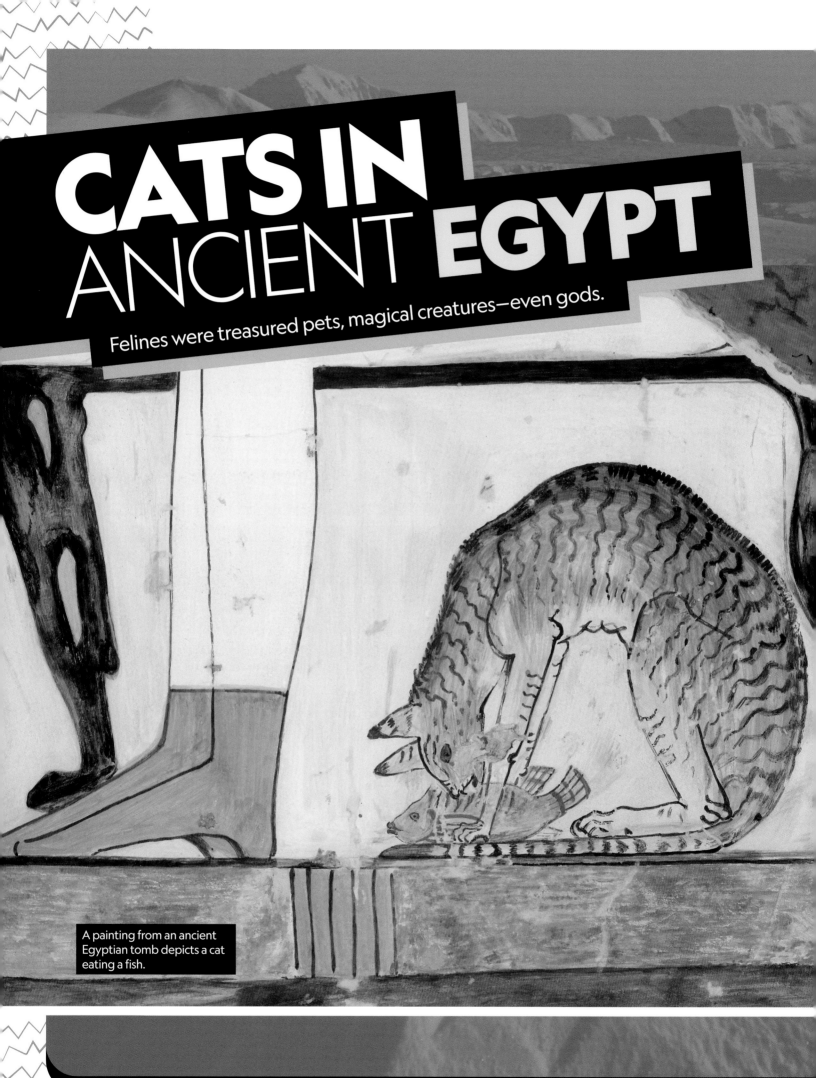

CATS IN ANCIENT EGYPT

Felines were treasured pets, magical creatures—even gods.

A painting from an ancient Egyptian tomb depicts a cat eating a fish.

>>> IN ANCIENT EGYPT, KILLING A CAT WAS A CRIME PUNISHABLE BY DEATH.

In the earliest drawings of cats in ancient Egyptian art, they are workers that hunt rats. But by 1500 B.C., pictures showed cats wearing collars and sitting under the dinner table. Wealthy Egyptians lavished their furry friends with jewels and fed them gourmet food. After their cat died, many people mummified it so their pet could join them in the afterlife—and everyone in the household shaved their eyebrows in mourning.

But domestic cats weren't just cozy companions: One was a deity. Bastet, the goddess of home, fertility, and childbirth, was a cat—or sometimes, a cat-headed woman. Worshippers believed that she protected them against evil spirits and disease.

Egyptian cat mummy, circa 400 B.C.

Egyptian statue of a cat representing the goddess Bastet

BIG HOUSE CATS

For pharaohs, the rulers of ancient Egypt, the bigger the cat, the better. They tamed cheetahs and kept them as pets. Many of the world's elite, from Italian nobles to Russian princes, made house pets out of these wild cats. The Mughal emperor Akbar the Great kept tamed cheetahs that he used to hunt antelope.

WINTER'S TALE

SUPER JAGUAR

I ALWAYS SAY THAT I DIDN'T CHOOSE TO PHOTOGRAPH BIG CATS; BIG CATS CHOSE ME. AND IT ALL STARTED WITH A JAGUAR.

My first big wildlife assignment sent me to the top of a mountain in Guatemala to photograph an almost magical, iridescent green-blue bird, the quetzal. One night, an animal was sniffing loudly outside the door of my cabin. I was alone. I put a chair up against the door. I grabbed my walkie-talkie and radioed a biologist who lived down the mountain and had been helping me. He was in a restaurant, and when I told him what I'd heard, a bunch of people started laughing. "Don't worry, Steve, it's only *un pantera negra*—a black jaguar." I spent most of that night wide awake. The next day, as I sat in the forest, a large animal crashed down from a tree limb. I glimpsed the cat as it disappeared into the forest.

My next story was on jaguars. That was 25 years ago.

I spent months trying to photograph this elusive cat. I set up remote cameras in thick jungle in Belize and got a few not-so-great pictures. In the rainforest, the cats don't always follow the same trails, making it impossible to predict where they will go. So I went to Costa Rica and set up my camera traps on a beach where jaguars feasted on nesting sea turtles. Again, no pictures. I never spied one, though I saw plenty of paw prints.

Finally, I flew to Brazil to work with a scientist who studied jaguars in the remote Pantanal wetlands. And I saw cats! The best way to look for them was by boat. There were few roads, and jaguars hunted and swam in the rivers that flowed everywhere. Sometimes they launched themselves off a bank into the water in pursuit of a caiman, a crocodile-like reptile and their favorite meal. I captured this cat midair; I call him Super Jaguar.

Some 95 percent of the Pantanal is privately owned by cattle ranchers and farmers, so jaguars were forced into conflict with people. When livestock died, jaguars were often blamed, even though that animal may have had a disease, been bitten by a snake, or encountered some other mishap.

I asked National Geographic to pay for satellite collars so that scientist Sandra Cavalcanti could put them on the cats. She was able to show ranchers that their jaguar neighbors were usually not responsible for their losses. It convinced some to not kill jaguars.

After I published my jaguar story, ecotourism grew in some parts of the Pantanal because it's the one place where you can actually see the cats. Soon, local people were making money working in hotels, serving as guides, or hosting tourists at their ranches. They realized that jaguars were even more valuable than their cows. One study in 2017 estimated that each jaguar was worth $108,000 a year in ecotourism income.

I've been back many times since. On my last visit, I saw 10 different jaguars in one day—a new record for me. In places that bring in tourists, jaguars are thriving.

A Sumatran tiger stalks the rainforest on the island of Sumatra, in Indonesia.

CHAPTER SEVEN

CHALLENGES FACING BIG CATS

>>> **CATLIKE ANIMALS HAVE WALKED OUR EARTH FOR 30 MILLION YEARS.** People have long admired and even worshipped them. But now humans pose the biggest threat to all big cats. Human activities, from cutting down forests to poaching, have taken a toll on their numbers. Many wild cat species are at risk of extinction. But if we learn about the challenges they face and take action, we can protect them. With a safe home and enough food to eat and water to drink, cats can bounce back because they reproduce well: One tigress can give birth to 15 cubs in her lifetime!

SHARED THREATS

Big cats live in different habitats across four continents, but their survival is threatened by many of the same things.

>>> HUMANS CONVERT BIG CATS' HOMELANDS INTO EVERYTHING FROM VILLAGES AND RANCHES TO FACTORIES AND ROADS, PUSHING CATS INTO SMALLER AND SMALLER LIVING QUARTERS. When forests are cut down by loggers or by local people who need wood to cook with, tigers lose their home. Climate change causes drought that leaves cats thirsty and generates extra-intense storms that flood whole areas. Poachers illegally hunt cats to sell their pelts and other parts or to sell cubs as pets. Hunters also kill other wild animals for meat; many of these species are food for big cats. Without sufficient prey, they sometimes go after livestock—and ranchers may take revenge on them.

It's important for biologists and conservationists to understand these threats so they can come up with solutions that allow cats and people to peacefully coexist. Here are the biggest problems threatening each big cat.

CUBS POACHED AND SOLD AS PETS

RETALIATION FOR LIVESTOCK ATTACKS

PROXIMITY TO HUMAN SETTLEMENTS

LEGAL TROPHY HUNTING

LAND USED FOR FARMING AND RANCHING

CAPTURE FOR ZOOS AND BREEDERS

MINING

LOGGING

DEVELOPMENT

ILLEGAL HUNTING

CLIMATE CHANGE

LOSS OF WILD PREY

REINTRODUCTION OF WOLVES

ROADS AND TRANSPORTATION

TIGER

LION

CHEETAH

JAGUAR

LEOPARD

COUGAR

SNOW LEOPARD

TACKLING THE
TIGER TRADE

It's illegal to kill tigers or remove them from their natural habitat because they are an endangered species. But in many countries, laws are weak and penalties are not well enforced. This makes the illegal international wildlife trade a low-risk, high-profit business.

Traditional Medicine

Throughout history, Asian cultures have revered tigers for their beauty, strength, and power. For millennia, medicine men believed the cats had magical powers and could heal people. Traditional Chinese medicine, which dates back at least 3,000 years, uses nearly every part of the tiger, from nose to tail, in some kind of treatment.

While there's no scientific evidence that they work, tiger medicines have been prescribed to treat epilepsy, baldness, ulcers, toothaches, fevers, joint pain, headaches, and other health issues. They were once thought to prevent nightmares. Even though Asian countries have adopted science-based medicine, many people still buy traditional remedies. Tiger bones are the most sought after part, used in an expensive "tiger bone wine" tonic.

A Prized Commodity

Tigers are also coveted for their beautiful skins, which decorate homes and offices. Their teeth and claws are made into jewelry. Live cats are sold to zoos and captive breeders.

Preserved tiger heads and skins seized by the U.S. Fish and Wildlife Service

Rangers out on patrol in Zakouma National Park, Chad

MUSK AND TIGER-BONE PLAST
辟香虎骨膏

虎骨膏

Tiger bone remedies that were illegally trafficked into the United States

PET CHEETAHS

Pharaohs, shahs, princes, and other nobles of the ancient world kept cheetahs as exotic pets. Owning them was a status symbol. The cats were captured in the wild and used for hunting, and their populations in Asia dropped dramatically. Cheetah cubs are still in high demand today. But in 2017, the United Arab Emirates imposed harsh penalties for smuggling or owning big cats: up to a $136,000 fine and six months behind bars. Conservationists hope that other countries will pass similar laws.

BY THE NUMBERS

How many big cats remain in the wild today? They often live in remote places, so no one knows for sure. Biologists use satellite collars, cameras, computer models, and in-the-field sightings to count them. Here are the best estimates for big cat populations today, along with information on where they live.

Lion

STATUS: Vulnerable in Africa; endangered in India; critically endangered in West Africa

ESTIMATED POPULATION: About 25,000

CURRENT TERRITORY: African lions live in 28 countries. Asiatic lions live in one Asian country.

CHANGE IN RANGE: Lions no longer live in 95 percent of their historic range.

Tiger

STATUS: Endangered

ESTIMATED POPULATION: Less than 4,000

CURRENT TERRITORY: Tigers live in 11 Asian countries, with healthy breeding populations in eight of them.

CHANGE IN RANGE: Tigers no longer live in 96 percent of their historic range.

Jaguar

STATUS: Near threatened

ESTIMATED POPULATION: 100,000

CURRENT TERRITORY: Jaguars live in 18 Latin American countries from Mexico to Argentina.

CHANGE IN RANGE: Jaguars no longer live in 40 percent of their historic range.

Cougar

STATUS: Least concern

ESTIMATED POPULATION: 100,000

CURRENT TERRITORY: Cougars live in 28 countries from the United States to Chile.

CHANGE IN RANGE: Cougars no longer live in 27 percent of their historic range.

Leopard

STATUS: Vulnerable, endangered (in Central Asia and Sri Lanka); critically endangered (in the Middle East, Russia, and the Indonesian island of Java)

ESTIMATED POPULATION: Not available (There aren't reliable global population estimates because leopards are elusive and their range covers vast areas.)

CURRENT TERRITORY: 62 countries in Asia and Africa

CHANGE IN RANGE: Worldwide, leopards no longer live in 65 percent of their historic range; in Asia, they have lost 85 percent of their former territory.

Snow Leopard

STATUS: Vulnerable

ESTIMATED POPULATION: 4,000 to 10,000

CURRENT TERRITORY: Snow leopards live in 12 Asian countries.

CHANGE IN RANGE: Unknown

Cheetah

STATUS: Vulnerable; critically endangered in Asia and North Africa

ESTIMATED POPULATION: 7100

CURRENT TERRITORY: Unknown

CHANGE IN RANGE: Cheetahs no longer live in 91 percent of their historic range.

Moment of AHHH!?!

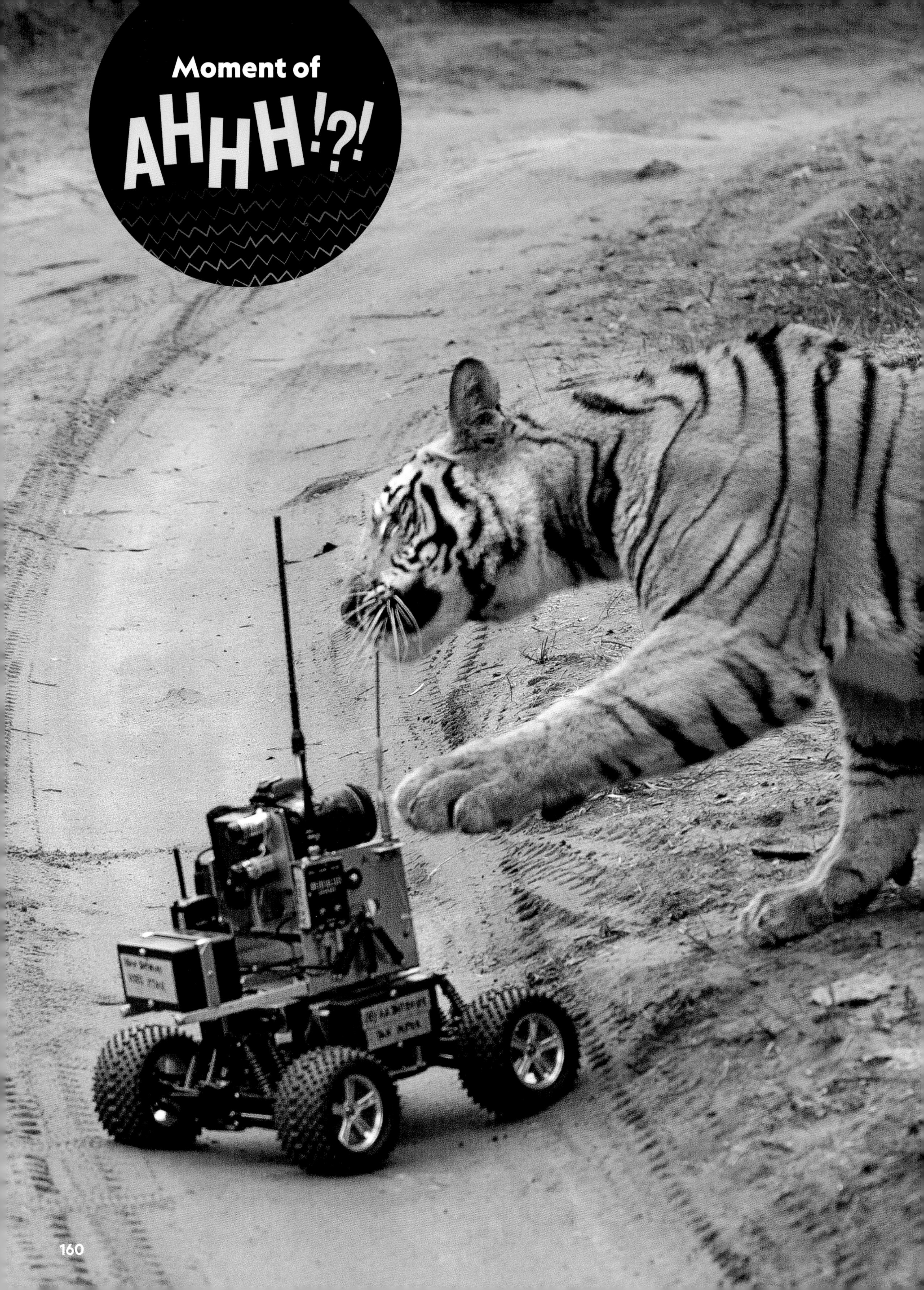

"You can't get a close-up of a tiger—they're too dangerous. So the engineers at National Geographic built me a remote-controlled camera car that I operated from my Jeep. I wanted to photograph three almost-grown 14-month-old cubs in India. The two males were afraid, but this female was curious: She sniffed the car and swatted at it, and I got good pictures of her in action!"

—Steve Winter

BIG BITES

The *Tyrannosaurus rex* roar in the movie *Jurassic Park* was made by combining a baby elephant's squeal, an alligator's gurgle, **AND A TIGER'S SNARL.**

South African giant bullfrogs, which can weigh up to 4.5 pounds (2 kg), sometimes **ATTACK AND BITE LIONS.**

Big cats, like house cats, **HAVE A "RIGHTING REFLEX":** When they're jumping or falling, they twist their bodies in midair, usually landing on their feet.

Cusco, the capital of the ancient Inca empire in what is now Peru, was designed in **THE SHAPE OF A COUGAR.**

At birth, a jaguar cub weighs about as much as **A LOAF OF BREAD.**

In a survey of 50,000 people in 73 countries, the tiger was the **WORLD'S FAVORITE ANIMAL.**

Researchers in India discovered that leopards are afraid of humans—and playing music on a mobile phone as you walk will **KEEP THEM AT A DISTANCE.**

Male house cats almost always **PREFER TO USE THEIR LEFT PAWS,** while females prefer to use their right paws.

When cats lick themselves, **THEY'RE NOT JUST GROOMING:** Chemicals in cat saliva protect wounds from infection and speed up healing.

Cougars are more closely related **TO HOUSE CATS** than to lions.

BEHIND THE SCENES WITH
WILDLIFE DETECTIVES

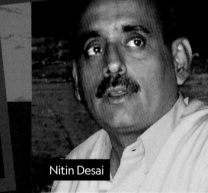

Nitin Desai

Belinda Wright

How do you stop someone from poaching big cats or illegally selling endangered species on the black market? Sometimes you go undercover.

>>> BELINDA WRIGHT, THE FOUNDER OF THE WILDLIFE PROTECTION SOCIETY OF INDIA, AND ONE OF ITS DIRECTORS, NITIN DESAI, HAVE HELPED POLICE CATCH POACHERS AND UNRAVEL ILLEGAL TRADE NETWORKS. They give us the inside scoop on wildlife trafficking and how they help stop it.

WHY DO PEOPLE COMMIT WILDLIFE CRIMES, INCLUDING POACHING AND SELLING BIG CATS?

WRIGHT: Selling wildlife [parts and live animals] brings in a lot of money! And even if you get caught, in many countries the penalties are light, so it is a low-risk crime.

WHAT ARE THESE TRAFFICKED CATS USED FOR?

DESAI: Parts are used to make clothing, home decorations, traditional medicines, wine tonics, jewelry, and good luck charms. Wild cats are also trafficked for zoos and the illegal pet trade. There is big demand, especially in Southeast Asia.

WHAT KINDS OF CHARGES ARE BROUGHT AGAINST PEOPLE COMMITTING WILDLIFE CRIMES?

WRIGHT: The illegal trade in wildlife is one of the most profitable crimes in the world, worth billions of dollars a year. But laws vary widely from country to country—from just a small fine to a jail sentence. Enforcement is generally weak, and many poachers and dealers get away with it.

HOW DO YOU FIND OUT WHO THE POACHERS AND WILDLIFE TRAFFICKERS ARE? AND HOW DO YOU CATCH THEM?

DESAI: Most poachers are part of organized gangs. They move around and target places with poor enforcement. So we track down poachers and wildlife traffickers through our wide network of informants. We gather information to hopefully stop them before they kill, or to catch them if they have. We pay people for tip-offs.

WHAT ARE SOME OF THE TOOLS YOU USE TO CATCH A BIG CAT TRAFFICKER?

WRIGHT: Since most wildlife criminals are repeat offenders, our huge wildlife crime database is an invaluable tool to help track down and follow suspects. We also use hidden cameras and recordings to help gather evidence. The devices are usually worn under our clothes or installed in a backpack or bag. Cell phone locations and records can be accessed by the enforcement authorities and used to identify criminal networks, link them to crimes, and reveal their locations. Using our knowledge and database, we often assist the authorities with their investigations.

DO YOU MAKE ARRESTS?

DESAI: We work closely with police, park rangers, and customs agents and always notify them on "active" leads. We do investigations, but they make arrests, and sometimes we assist them in the field.

To help others investigate wildlife crime and convict criminals, we teach park guards how to collect evidence at a crime scene, and we run workshops for customs officials and judges who may not be experts on wildlife trade or endangered species.

YOU'VE GONE UNDERCOVER TO CATCH WILDLIFE TRAFFICKERS. WAS IT DANGEROUS?

WRIGHT: Yes, it's dangerous. Careful preparation, good backup, and communication are important. But a successful undercover operation depends on convincing the wildlife trafficker that you're really a buyer and they can trust you. We need to remain calm and use the best tool we have—our brainpower—to avoid ending up in a dangerous situation. In case something goes wrong, we have exit strategies in place.

HOW CAN WILDLIFE CRIME BE STOPPED?

DESAI: By improving intelligence-led enforcement and coordination between agencies, and by providing better resources and training. At present, the prosecution of wildlife court cases is poor and conviction rates, which should act as a strong deterrent, are low.

IS MOST TIGER POACHING DONE TO MAKE TRADITIONAL MEDICINES?

DESAI: Tiger poaching for skins and traditional medicines has been relentless for the past 30 years. But that is changing, with a disturbing new trend. Most of the tigers killed in early 2021 in India were slain because they came near villages or were captured in traps set for bushmeat—deer, boar, or other animals that people eat.

HAS PROGRESS BEEN MADE IN STOPPING WILDLIFE CRIMES? WHAT GIVES YOU HOPE?

WRIGHT: There is a lot more interest and knowledge about this, with more news stories publicizing it. Some exceptional wildlife crime enforcement officers are catching criminals. Governments are investing in wildlife conservation efforts.

India, which is home to most of the world's tigers, has 981 protected areas. They include 52 tiger reserves that cover 28,000 square miles (72,500 sq km). That's about the size of Ireland. But the tigers themselves give us hope. They are a resilient species, and in recent years tigers have been turning up in unexpected places, often outside protected areas. They continue to surprise us!

MYTHS BUSTED

Separate fact from fiction by finding out which of these beliefs about big cats are true and which ones belong in a comic book.

MYTH: WHITE TIGERS ARE ALBINOS.

False!

White tigers are a rare variety of Bengal tiger. Albino animals and white tigers both carry genetic mutations. Albinos lack pigment in their skin, eyes, and hair or fur, and they have pink eyes. White tigers carry a different genetic mutation that gives them their milky white fur, and they usually have blue or green eyes. Both parents must carry this rare gene to produce white cubs. Because we see white tigers in zoos or on TV, it seems like they're common, but they're not. Only a few have ever been spotted in the wild in India, and none have been seen for 60 years. Why are they so rare? A tiger's brownish orange coat and stripes camouflage them from potential prey. A glowing white predator would have a tough time trying to catch its dinner!

In 1960, the first blue-eyed white tiger arrived in the U.S. from India. Mohini, a female, was donated to the Smithsonian's National Zoo in Washington, D.C. The tiger and her offspring were inbred (meaning bred with close relatives), and two were sent to the Cincinnati Zoo in Ohio, U.S.A. They were big moneymakers: From 1974 to 1990, that zoo bred 91 white tiger cubs and sold them across the United States for up to $60,000 each. White cubs attracted tourists to circus acts and zoos. But inbreeding can cause deformities and health problems, so in 2012, the Association of Zoos and Aquariums banned its members from breeding white tigers. Only unaccredited roadside zoos still breed them.

MYTH: A LIGER IS A CROSS BETWEEN A LION AND TIGER.

True!

But this isn't an animal you'd ever see in the wild, as these hybrid mixes don't exist in nature. Roadside zoo owners breed female tigers and male lions to create ligers because they attract tourists. These hybrid cats often have serious health problems. They suffer from gigantism, growing to a monstrous size, larger than either of their parents. That's because a lion mother gives her offspring a gene that helps control their growth; with a tiger mother, ligers lack this gene. Standing on their hind legs, ligers can measure up to 11 feet (3.4 m) tall and weigh nearly 1,000 pounds (454 kg)—about the size of a polar bear.

MYTH: TASMANIAN TIGERS ARE EXTINCT.

True

But the name is misleading. Yes, the Tasmanian tiger is extinct, but it wasn't actually a tiger. It was a carnivorous marsupial that raised its babies in a pouch, like a kangaroo. Among scientists, this animal is known as a thylacine, but it probably got the name "Tasmanian tiger" because of tigerlike stripes on its back. It once lived across Australia, Tasmania, and New Guinea, but the last one died in captivity in 1936. Scientists have considered using stored DNA to one day clone it and try to bring it back to life, but that's not likely to happen. The DNA is poor quality, and cloning is a very complicated process.

WINTER'S TALE

TAKING CARE OF TIGERS

DON'T WORRY, THIS TIGRESS ISN'T DEAD. These scientists, who I call the Thai Tiger Team, study Indochinese tigers in Thailand. After capturing and tranquilizing this cat, they put a rubber collar fitted with a satellite transmitter on her. For the next two years, it sent GPS locations to their laptops so the team could track where the tigress went.

My goal throughout my career has been to capture the beauty, intelligence, and behaviors of the animals I photograph, but I also need to tell their story. That includes everything from the threats they face to the people who study and try to save them.

I had the incredible opportunity to camp with the team in Huai Kha Khaeng Wildlife Sanctuary. They'd set up a snare, baited it with meat, and checked it every two hours. The tigress came at night, and we rushed over. The researchers used a dart to give the tigress a sedative, and she went to sleep, though her eyes were still open.

The scientists sprang into action just as the sun rose. Some monitored the cat's heartbeat, weighed and measured her, and took blood samples while others put the collar on. She was huge—and gorgeous.

I spent four months in the park, living in a cabin most of the time. This was thick, lush jungle, almost completely undisturbed by humans. It's part of the largest remaining tropical forest in Southeast Asia. It's also a stronghold for some of the last of these endangered Indochinese tigers. Only a few hundred are left in the wild.

Scientists have worked in this park for decades, which makes these cats some of the best studied tigers in the world. Even so, biologists still didn't know much about their daily lives. For this study, they wanted to find out how much space a mother needed to hunt for herself and her cubs. The size of a cat's territory changes from place to place, according to how much prey is available. It's important information for conservation.

Another reason why the Thai Tiger Team captured and collared female tigers was to better protect them. Knowing where tigers live in this huge park helped rangers patrol the right areas. Poachers are a real threat: Tiger parts are worth a lot of money in the illegal wildlife trade, especially in Asia, although killing this endangered species is against the law.

While I was there, the team started an elite patrol, with park rangers trained by army and police officers. The guards collect and share data on their cell phones through a "SMART Patrol" app, and it's working: Not one tiger has been killed for years.

Now tigers are doing what cats do when they're safe and have enough to eat: having cubs! In 2007, researchers counted 46 adult tigers in the park. By 2020, there were 79. This picture documented a happy moment. While examining this tigress, the team made an exciting discovery: She was pregnant. The man on the right is listening to the cubs' heartbeats inside her belly.

CHAPTER EIGHT

BE A BIG CAT DEFENDER

>>> LEAPING FROM TALL CLIFFS IN A SINGLE BOUND. GOING UNDERCOVER FOR A SNEAK ATTACK. Swiping prey with one powerful paw. With their super strength, stealth, and size, big cats are among the superheroes of the animal kingdom. They have some human superheroes working on their side, too! Scientists, conservationists, and activists across the globe are working to protect and save these magnificent animals by studying them in the field—and by finding ways for people to safely live with and benefit from their big cat neighbors. Let's meet some of the people who are saving big cats and learn how you can help, too!

A jaguar leaps into a river in Brazil in pursuit of a caiman.

MAKING SPACE FOR
BIG CATS

>>> **WILD CATS ONCE LIVED ACROSS THE PLANET.** But over the last 100 years, today's big cats have lost huge chunks of their former territory. These wide-ranging felines need big spaces to live, hunt, and raise their cubs. National parks and reserves are some of their last strongholds.

INDIA'S TIGER
RESERVES

Throughout history, India's Bengal tigers have been a target for hunters. The cats were slain during elaborate royal hunts staged for Indian royalty and British nobles, and they were stalked by big-game hunters and wildlife traders. A fashion craze for fur coats in the 1960s also took a huge toll. When Rudyard Kipling wrote *The Jungle Book* in 1894, about 40,000 tigers roamed India. By 1971, only about 1,800 were left. But in 1973, Prime Minister Indira Gandhi launched Project Tiger. Killing tigers became a crime. She established nine tiger reserves and hired guards to patrol the land. Today, there are 52 reserves, many of which are former royal hunting grounds that now give tigers safe haven. With this protection, tigers have bounced back: As of 2019, more than 2,967 Bengals roam India. That's more than two-thirds of all the tigers that remain in the wild.

Park rangers protect tigers from poachers in India's Bandhavgarh Tiger Reserve.

A SUPER SANCTUARY FOR
ASIATIC LIONS

The last wild Asiatic lions live in and around Gir National Park in India. A century ago, fewer than 50 remained after years of habitat loss and hunting. Now there are about 674, thanks to the real-life superheroes who protect them: the wildlife rescuers at the Team Wildlife Division, Sasan-Gir, Gujarat Forest Department. This group tracks the cats and acts as peacekeepers with local communities when lions come into villages or kill livestock. While these Asiatic lions are still endangered, their numbers continue to rise.

Gir National Park Rangers ride on motorbikes to track lions.

Park rangers on duty in South Africa

PARKS FOR
LIONS, LEOPARDS, AND CHEETAHS

Many developing countries can't afford to protect their wildlife. So 20 years ago, a conservation organization called African Parks brainstormed a unique way to help. In partnership with local governments, this organization runs 19 national parks in 11 African nations, many of which are home to lions, leopards, and cheetahs. For these parks to thrive, local people must benefit, too. African Parks gives them jobs, sets up medical clinics, and supports schools. To protect wildlife against heavily armed poachers, it has deployed about 1,000 rangers and canine units. It is also "rewilding" animals to places where they've disappeared. For example, nearly 5,000 animals of 16 different species were moved to Majete Wildlife Reserve in Malawi. A lion pride in Akagera National Park in Rwanda has tripled in size since seven lions were reintroduced there in 2015. This teamwork has proved to be a success: The numbers of big cats, elephants, giraffes, and many other species in these parks keep growing!

CHANGING
CLIMATE

Every wild cat—and every living thing on Earth—is under threat from climate change. Over the last century, burning fossil fuels like coal and oil has increased the amount of carbon dioxide in the atmosphere. Our planet is warming, and intense storms, flooding, and drought have become more frequent. For snow leopards, rapidly rising temperatures on the Tibetan Plateau could make their habitat unusable—and that's where more than half of these elusive cats live. In India and Bangladesh, rising sea levels threaten tigers living in coastal mangroves. Lions in Africa's Serengeti have suffered through both drought and floods. Conservationists are working to create more national parks and reserves for cats so they have places to go if climate change affects their habitat or prey. And experts are working to transition the world to clean, renewable energy sources.

Moment of AHHH!?!

"Some people might be scared if they came upon a wild jaguar with its mouth wide open—even if it was just yawning like this one! I was not far away, shooting pictures from a boat as this cat woke from its nap by the river. But there was no reason to be afraid. Jaguars almost never attack people. They just need respect, space, and protection."

—Steve Winter

SUPER SOLUTIONS

>>> LIVING WITH BIG CATS AS NEIGHBORS IS CHALLENGING: THEY ARE, AFTER ALL, TOP PREDATORS.

Though it's rare, they do sometimes attack or kill people. And losing livestock to a big cat can be devastating for families who rely on these animals for their income and their survival. But conservationists have created win-win programs that benefit local communities and save big cats. And park guards are wildlife defenders who are working on the front lines to protect forests from illegal loggers and animals from poachers. They are securing a future for big cats!

Highly trained rangers patrol Huai Kha Khaeng National Park in Thailand to protect animals from poachers.

Phone Patrol

Poaching for illegal trade is a top threat for big cats around the world. Guarding them is a dangerous job, and thousands of rangers put their lives on the line every day to protect wildlife. There aren't enough guards to patrol the cats' vast habitats, but with just a cell phone, rangers can pinpoint high-risk areas. They input information into a data collection app, including wildlife sightings, tracks—such as hoofprints, paw prints, or footprints—illegally logged trees, and the presence of animal traps or other signs of poaching. Park managers then use this information to adjust patrol tactics and strategies. Artificial intelligence can use the data to predict where poachers might go next. It's been incredibly successful: Now there is less poaching and more animals in many of these habitats.

A veterinarian vaccinates cattle in Pakistan.

Safeguarding Snow Leopards

Herders in remote villages in the Himalaya in Pakistan are some of the snow leopard's best friends. Protecting these cats—once considered a threat to their yak, sheep, and goats—now brings in needed income. Some of this money comes from tourism: Trekkers stay in the herders' homes when hiking through these mountains. Another program helps them grow their herds. Since disease kills five times more livestock than snow leopards do, the conservation organization Snow Leopard Trust brings in veterinarians to vaccinate farm animals for owners who pledge to safeguard the cats. Herders now lose far fewer animals to disease.

Crafty Conservation

There aren't many ways to earn money if you live deep in the forest, so some people resort to poaching. A local organization, Dhonk Crafts, found a way for women who live near India's Ranthambore Tiger Reserve to bring in cash. It trains them to make traditional handcrafted items and helps them sell their products online and to tourists who visit the reserve. This community now bands together to safeguard the park's tigers.

DOGS ON GUARD

Cheetahs sometimes prey on livestock, and farmers retaliate by killing them. So in 1994, the Cheetah Conservation Fund started breeding and selling Anatolian shepherd dogs to farmers in Namibia. These huge dogs have protected sheep from wolves and bears for 6,000 years in Turkey. They're not herd dogs. Instead, they grow up living with goats or sheep and guard them like family. The dogs can handle a herd of 200 with virtually no losses, so farmers can rely on them to protect their livestock, and the cheetahs' lives are spared. The Wildlife Conservation Society is also deploying these canine guardians in Argentina to protect herds from cougars, and from Geoffroy's, pampas, and Andean cats.

Anatolian shepherd

SAVING BIG CATS BY PROTECTING LIVESTOCK

Livestock can become prey for cats, and people are finding ways to help the animals coexist.

>>> WHEN BIG CATS ARE HUNGRY, THEY NEED TO EAT. BUT IN MANY PLACES, THEIR PREY IS DISAPPEARING. People eat some of the same animals that cats do, like deer and antelope. Their farms take over the cats' habitat, too, and their livestock—sheep, yaks, cows, and goats—make an easy meal for a hungry cat on the prowl. But losing these animals is a real hardship for the families that own them because livestock provides milk, meat, wool, and income. Sometimes farmers and ranchers retaliate by killing cats. So conservationists are finding ways to protect livestock—and protect cats.

A livestock enclosure in Masai Mara, Kenya

Human-Lion Conflict

Lions in Tanzania sometimes take down cattle that are owned by Indigenous Maasai people. A local conservation organization, African People & Wildlife, partnered with the Maasai to find ways for them to coexist with these large predators.

Big Consequences

East Africa's Maasai people rely on livestock to survive, says Laly Lichtenfeld, a National Geographic Explorer who cofounded African People & Wildlife. "If you have a cow that has been killed by a lion, that hurts. It makes people angry," she says. The cow's owner may spear or shoot the cat.

Or sometimes, Maasai herders put poison in the carcass of a dead cow, hoping the pride will come back to feed again. If the lions return, all of them could die. Other scavenger species—like vultures, jackals, and hyenas—may also be poisoned.

These cat-human conflicts are a major threat to big cats across the globe, from snow leopards that sometimes kill yak in the Himalaya to jaguars that may prey on cattle in Brazil to cougars that go after sheep in Wyoming, U.S.A.

A herdsman in Kenya stands next to a cow that was killed by a lion.

Laly Lichtenfeld (left) delivers wire for a living wall in Tanzania.

Brainstorming a Solution

Lichtenfeld and the Maasai brainstormed a way to protect livestock that also protects lions, leopards, cheetahs, and other predators. Here's how it works: The Maasai had always put their animals in corrals at night, but the fences didn't keep intruders out. So African People & Wildlife is replacing low fences with tall, predator-proof corrals. Lichtenfeld calls them "living walls" because they're made from fast-growing trees and chain-link fencing.

So far, the organization has planted 184,000 trees to build 1,327 living walls. And they work. "It's amazing how tolerant people still are in East Africa of living with large mammals—and potentially dangerous ones," Lichtenfeld says. Her organization has also recruited a rapid-response team of 50 local "warriors for wildlife" to respond to human-wildlife conflicts.

BEHIND THE SCENES WITH
BITTU SAHGAL

For 22 years, Bittu Sahgal has been on a mission to teach kids in India about nature, conservation, and their national animal, the tiger.

>>> ABOUT 600 ELEMENTARY AND MIDDLE SCHOOLS ACROSS INDIA TAKE PART IN BITTU SAHGAL'S "KIDS FOR TIGERS" PROGRAM EACH YEAR. It brings sports stars, celebrities, and conservationists into classrooms, and it also takes kids out into wildlife reserves. Many of them live in cities and had never been in a forest or seen animals in the wild before. Kids become tiger ambassadors and wildlife defenders. They write letters to India's prime minister and other government officials, and they have collected more than two million signatures on petitions in a single year to save tigers. Kids also participate in public tiger festivals. They march in rallies of up to 2,000 kids, carrying signs, with their faces painted like tigers or dressed in tiger costumes. More than a million Kids for Tigers conservationists are now helping save India's last wild lands, its wildlife, and its tigers.

Middle school students march at a rally in Chandrapur, India, to raise awareness about tiger conservation.

Fifth and sixth graders painted their faces to rally for tigers.

WHY IS IT IMPORTANT TO TEACH KIDS ABOUT THE IMPORTANCE OF TIGERS?

SAHGAL: The tiger is a metaphor for all of nature. What we say is this: No one can save the tiger if we don't save its forest, its habitat. And if you save the forest, you save every single species living in this forest, from small to large. And forests trap carbon and slow climate change, helping prevent floods and droughts. They also feed clean water to more than 600 rivers that give us water to drink. So if you save the tiger, you save yourself.

WHEN DID YOU BECOME INTERESTED IN TIGER CONSERVATION?

SAHGAL: As a child I lived in Kolkata, and the only tigers I ever saw were at the zoo. When I asked why they were in prison, I was told they were dangerous, and I believed that to be true. When I was in my early 20s, I saw my first wild tigers, a mother and cub in the Kanha Tiger Reserve. The cats ignored me. My late friend Manglu Baiga, a tribal wise man, explained that the tiger was not only safe to be around, but also a protector of the forest. I fell in love with tigers ... and everything wild.

WHAT KINDS OF ACTIVITIES ARE PART OF THE KIDS FOR TIGERS PROGRAM?

SAHGAL: We take kids out into tiger reserves, show nature films, run nature camps, and hold Tiger Fest rallies and debates. They become tiger ambassadors and conduct signature campaigns, and we get celebrities, conservationists, and journalists to come to their schools and talk to the kids about protecting nature.

WHY IS IT IMPORTANT FOR CHILDREN TO LEARN ABOUT CONSERVATION?

SAHGAL: Over the last 50 or so years, we've reduced the physical space for tigers. Half of all tiger habitats are gone forever, turned into towns, mines, etc. Kids have a natural affinity for animals and nature. When we connect kids to the wild, it rekindles a flame lying dormant within them. We equip them with the most powerful tool for their own future survival: awe and respect for nature. And I can't think of anyone with a greater right to ask for a better tomorrow than children. We wanted to give kids a voice, give them a sense of confidence in tomorrow, and tell them that you can make a difference! We can—we will—save the tiger!

TEST YOUR BIG CAT SAVVY

Do you think you know big cats? It's time to test your knowledge!
See if you can correctly pair each question with the right cat—or cats!

1 Which cat is the **FASTEST?**
(Hint: See pages 62–63.)

2 Which cat has markings on the back of its ears that look like **A PAIR OF EYES?**
(Hint: See pages 58–59.)

3 Which cat can jump the **FARTHEST?**
(Hint: See pages 64–65.)

4 Which two cats **LOVE THE WATER** and are amazing long-distance swimmers?
(Hint: See pages 118–119.)

5 Which cat has the most **POWERFUL BITE** relative to its size?
(Hint: See pages 50–51.)

7

Which two big cats can have

BLUE OR GREEN EYES?

(Hint: See pages 56–57 and 166–167.)

9

Which big cat is the

BIGGEST?

(Hint: See pages 14–15.)

8

Which two cats have

THE WORD "GHOST"

as part of their nickname?

(Hint: See pages 20–21 and 34–35.)

10

Which cat's body is part of such

MYTHICAL CREATURES

as the griffin and the Sphinx?

(Hint: See pages 142–143.)

6

Which big cat has

semi-retractable claws

LIKE A DOG?

(Hint: See pages 46–47.)

ANSWERS: 1. Cheetah; 2. Tiger; 3. Snow leopard; 4. Jaguars and tigers; 5. Jaguar; 6. Cheetah; 7. Snow leopards and white tigers; 8. Snow leopards and cougars; 9. Tiger; 10. Lion

YOU CAN BE A BIG CAT HERO

You don't have to travel across the globe to be a big cat defender. There are a lot of things you can do from home, right now! Our imaginations are powerful, and our ideas and actions can make a difference. Check out the ways that you can help protect big cats, no matter where you live.

Bittu Sahgal marches with children in India to save the tigers—and nature.

Raise Your Voice

Laurie Marker, the woman who started the Cheetah Conservation Fund in Namibia, has advice on saving wildlife. "Animals need our help," she says. "Don't wait for somebody to do it! You can do anything!"

Bittu Sahgal says, "Speak up!" You can help conservation organizations gain support for new wildlife reserves, and you can encourage government leaders to approve and provide funding for them. Write letters to leaders in Congress and other U.S. or international officials. Ask them to support laws that protect wildlife, stop the illegal wildlife trade, and address climate change; or contact them about other environmental topics that are important to you.

Read

You've already done something to help big cats—you've learned more about them! By reading about big cats and other wildlife, you educate yourself about the threats to their survival, and you learn how your actions and choices can make a difference.

Avoid Going to Unaccredited Zoos

If you want to see big cats, research before you go. Roadside animal attractions and private zoos not accredited by the Association of Zoos and Aquariums or the Global Federation of Animal Sanctuaries can be dangerous or unhealthy places for big cats. Avoid attractions that offer hands-on contact with tiger cubs or other wild species.

Avoid Products Made With Palm Oil

By avoiding products made with palm oil, you send a message to manufacturers that you don't support cutting down rainforests for palm oil plantations. These rainforests are home to tigers, jaguars, leopards, and other wildlife. Read product labels: Palm oil is used in everything from pizza, bread, peanut butter, cookies, and energy bars to shampoo, soap, makeup, and cleaning products. And you can ask a parent or teacher to help you make sure other products you buy, like paper and items made of wood, didn't come from illegal logging.

In Sumatra, Indonesia, tiger habitat is deforested for palm oil plantations.

Start a Fundraiser

Have you ever held a bake sale or helped in some other way to raise money for a good cause? Why not do the same thing for wildlife? Find a reputable conservation organization, ask your parents or teachers to help you organize a fundraiser, and then donate the proceeds. Some smaller organizations working on the ground in big cat habitats or those that focus on a specific cat species often need the most help!

Spread the Word

Tell your family and friends all about big cats and the issues they face. By informing them, you are increasing awareness about big cat conservation!

WINTER'S TALE

SPARKING CHANGE

WILD CATS, BOTH BIG AND SMALL, ARE IN TROUBLE ACROSS THE GLOBE. ALMOST ALL ARE ENDANGERED.

They face many threats. Our growing human population has left them with little room to roam. And many people are unwilling to share land with these wide-ranging predators, and so they hunt them or their prey. Poachers target cats for their skins, claws, bones, and other parts, which they sell illegally for a lot of money. Cheetah cubs are taken from the wild and sold as pets, particularly in the countries around the Persian Gulf.

Climate change is raising temperatures and causing more intense storms and longer droughts, affecting the ecosystems where cats live. The Sundarbans mangroves in India and Bangladesh are slowly sinking into the Bay of Bengal as sea levels rise. Snow leopards may lose much of their habitat as their cold mountain homeland heats up.

But people across the planet are also working to save wildlife and the ecosystems that both animals and humans depend on for survival. For example, dozens of countries have joined a new "30×30 Initiative" to protect at least 30 percent of Earth's land and ocean by 2030. In 2021, the United Nations launched the Decade on Ecosystem Restoration program to prevent, stop, and reverse damage to ecosystems worldwide.

Another project, End Wildlife Crime, is trying to establish stronger global wildlife trade laws. Many countries now realize that wildlife trafficking is a serious crime, run by international criminal organizations. Wildlife rangers bravely fight to defend the animals in their reserves. The Thin Green Line Foundation raises money to send essential equipment and provide specialized training to rangers in 60 countries. The 2015 Paris Agreement is trying to limit global warming to less than 3.6°F (2°C) above levels from 150 years ago, before the industrial revolution brought heavy use of fossil fuels.

Conservation organizations are protecting land and working with local people to find ways they can live with wild cats as neighbors. They're building predator-proof corrals, paying people for livestock that cats have killed, and finding ways to bring money to local communities. In places where people have better schools and medical care, and can earn more income by protecting wildlife, animals are rebounding.

Government and religious leaders, scientists, conservationists, and citizens are speaking up and taking action on behalf of wildlife. And kids are, too! More than a million children in India are part of the Kids for Tigers movement to save tigers and their habitat. Sharon Guynup and I have found that our work as writers and photographers has had impact, from helping create a wildlife overpass in California, U.S.A., and a new tiger reserve in Myanmar to raising awareness about the abusive cub-petting industry and helping save jaguars.

We all can make a difference.

INDEX

Boldface indicates illustrations.

INDEX

CREDITS

CHAPTER 1: (snow BACKGROUND), Incredible Arctic/Shutterstock; (rainforest BACKGROUND), merrymuuu/Shutterstock; 4 (UP), Eric Isselee/Shutterstock; 4 (LO), clarst5/Shutterstock; 5, Dennis Jacobsen/Adobe Stock; 10 (Asiatic lion), Anup Shah/Nature Picture Library; 12-13, Irina Nedikova/Alamy Stock Photo; 13 (UP), Katja Forster/Shutterstock; 13 (CTR), vaclav/Adobe Stock; 13 (LO LE), Juniors Bildarchiv GmbH/Alamy Stock Photo; 13 (LO RT), Volodymyr Burdiak/Shutterstock; 15 (UP), Vladimir Medvedev/Nature Picture Library; 16, Edwin Giesbers/Nature Picture Library; 19 (LO), Anup Shah/Nature Picture Library; 20, Nick Garbutt/Minden Pictures; 25, Carlton Ward/National Geographic Image Collection; 28-29, Frans Lanting/National Geographic Image Collection; 33 (Asiatic lion), Anup Shah/Nature Picture Library; 34, Carlton Ward/National Geographic Image Collection; 35 (UP), Giri Cavale/Nature Picture Library; 35 (LO), Felis Images/Nature Picture Library; 36 (refrigerator), Todd Taulman/Adobe Stock; 36 (dog), Eric Isselee/Dreamstime; 36 (leopard), Eric Isselee/Shutterstock; 36 (lion), Eric Isselee/Shutterstock; 36 (laptop), zentilia/Shutterstock; 36 (tiger), apple2499/Shutterstock; 37 (snow leopard), Eric Isselee/Shutterstock; 37 (rabbit), Arlee.P/Shutterstock; 37 (cheetah), Eric Isselee/Shutterstock; 37 (jaguar), Anan Kaewkhammul/Shutterstock; 37 (milk), Kenishirotie/Shutterstock; 37 (skateboard), Heike Brauer/Shutterstock; 37 (domestic cat), dien/Shutterstock; 37 (cougar), Eric Isselee/Shutterstock; **CHAPTER 2:** 43 (UP), imagebroker/Adobe Stock; 43 (CTR), Frans Lanting/National Geographic Image Collection; 45 (UP), Anup Shah/Nature Picture Library; 46 (UP), Christophe Courteau/Nature Picture Library; 46 (LO), Suntisook.D/Shutterstock; 47 (UP), Robin Chittenden/FLPA/Minden Pictures; 47 (LO), Tony Heald/Nature Picture Library; 49 (UP RT), Michel & Christine Denis-Huot/Biosphoto; 55, Andy Rouse/Nature Picture Library; 57 (LO), Heinrich Van Den Berg/Dreamstime; 58, Philip Perry/FLPA/Minden Pictures; 59 (UP), Michel & Christine Denis-Huot/Biosphoto; 61 (UP), ZSSD/Minden Pictures; 61 (LO), Staffan Widstrand/Nature Picture Library; 62-63, Richard Du Toit/Minden Pictures; 63 (Asiatic Lion), Anup Shah/Nature Picture Library; 66, Peter Cairns/Nature Picture Library; 67 (CTR), Ben Cranke/Nature Picture Library; 67 (LO), Mary McDonald/Nature Picture Library; 67 (UP), Klein & Hubert/Nature Picture Library; 68 (LO), Ben Cranke/Minden Pictures; 68 (UP), Terry Whittaker/Nature Picture Library; 69 (UP), Sylvain Cordier/Biosphoto; 69 (LO LE), Sebastian Kennerknecht/Minden Pictures; 69 (LO RT), Roland Seitre/Minden Pictures; **CHAPTER 3:** 75 (UP), Michel & Christine Denis-Huot/Biosphoto; 77 (LO), Beverly Joubert/National Geographic Image Collection; 79 (CTR LE), Beverly Joubert/National Geographic Image Collection; 84-85, Will Burrard-Lucas/Nature Picture Library; 85 (LO), jim kruger/E+/Getty Images; 85 (UP), Sushil Chikane/Alamy Stock Photo; **CHAPTER 4:** 98 (UP), Heritage Image Partnership Ltd/Alamy Stock Photo; 99 (LO), Jessica Rinaldi/The Boston Globe via Getty Images; 99 (UP), Ivy Close Images/Alamy Stock Photo; 106, Nick Garbutt/Minden Pictures; 107 (wolf), Mari_art/Adobe Stock; 107 (coyote), Outdoorsman/Dreamstime; 107 (maned wolf), Anan Kaewkhammul/Shutterstock; 107 (black bear), Svetlana Foote/Shutterstock; 107 (jaguar), Anan Kaewkhammul/Shutterstock; 107 (grizzly bear), ducu59us/Shutterstock; 109 (polar bear), Agami/Adobe Stock; 109 (wolf), Holly Kuchera/Shutterstock; 109 (lion), Anup Shah/Nature Picture Library; 109 (cat), alex avol/Shutterstock; 109 (wild dog), ondrej prosicky/Adobe Stock; 109 (dragonfly), J. L. Levy/Shutterstock; 112 (marmot), Eric Isselée/Adobe Stock; 112 (ibex), Ali Alawartani/Adobe Stock; 112 (blue sheep), Agami/Adobe Stock; 112 (sambar deer), anankkml/Adobe Stock; 112 (Thompson's gazelle), stuporter/Adobe Stock; 112 (wild pig), Eric Isselée/Adobe Stock; 112 (guar), crbellette/Shutterstock; 112 (giraffe), Eric Isselee/Shutterstock; 112 (zebra), Anan Kaewkhammul/Shutterstock; 112 (African buffalo), Four Oaks/Shutterstock; 112-113 (blue plate), karandaev/Adobe Stock; 112-113 (green plate), missty/Adobe Stock; 112 (white plate), grey/Adobe Stock; 112-113 (white plate), sommai/Adobe Stock; 113 (tilapia), supia/Adobe Stock; 113 (arapaima fish), Ammit/Adobe Stock; 113 (impala), anankkml/Adobe Stock; 113 (tapir), Odua Images/Adobe Stock; 113 (hare), Jonathan Oberholster/Shutterstock; 113 (monkey), Eric Isselee/Shutterstock; 113 (rabbit), sonsedskaya/Shutterstock; 113 (caiman), reptiles4all/Shutterstock; 113 (rat), LiskaM/Shutterstock; 113 (mouse), Rudmer Zwerver/Shutterstock; 113 (white plate), sommai/Adobe Stock; **CHAPTER 5:** 119 (LO), Felis Images/Nature Picture Library; 122 (UP LE), Julian Schaldach/Adobe Stock; 122 (UP CTR), WLDavies/E+/Getty Images; 122 (CTR), ami mataraj/Shutterstock; 122 (UP RT), Eric Isselee/Shutterstock; 123 (LO RT), Marion Vollborn/BIA/Minden Pictures; 123 (UP LE), Ondrej Prosicky/BIA/Minden Pictures; 123 (UP RT), Hekla/Shutterstock; 126-127, Joel Sartore/National Geographic Image Collection; 127 (LO), Carlton Ward/National Geographic Image Collection; **CHAPTER 6:** 136-137, Photodisc; 138, Franco Tempesta; 139 (UP), Daniel Eskridge/Alamy Stock Photo; 139 (CTR), Millard H. Sharp/Science Source; 139 (LO), Reuters/Alamy Stock Photo; 140, Natural Visions/Alamy Stock Photo; 142, Iunstream/Alamy Stock Photo; 143 (UP), Fletcher Fund, 1940/Metropolitan Museum of Art; 143 (LO), Jeremy Pembrey/Alamy Stock Photo; 143 (CTR), Museo Archeologico Nazionale, Florence, Italy/Raffaello Bencini/Bridgeman Images; 146, Heritage Image Partnership Ltd/Alamy Stock Photo; 147 (LO), Brooklyn Museum of Art/Carll H. de Silver Fund/Bridgeman Images; 147 (UP), Luisa Ricciarini/Bridgeman Images; 148, Ashmolean Museum/Bridgeman Images; 149 (UP), Kenneth Garrett; 149 (CTR), Gift of Mrs. Frederick F. Thompson, 1915/Metropolitan Museum of Art; **CHAPTER 7:** 157 (LO), Vintage Images/Alamy Stock Photo; 162 (LO RT), Stu Porter/Shutterstock; 162 (UP RT), DM7/Shutterstock; 162 (UP LE), Anton Sorokin/Alamy Stock Photo; 162 (LO LE), PhotoHouse/Shutterstock; 163 (LO LE), Antonio Gravante/Shutterstock; 164 (LO RT), Ramki; 167 (LO), Les Archives Digitales/Alamy Stock Photo; **CHAPTER 8:** 173 (LO), Wildlife Division, Sasan-Gir/Gir National Park & Sanctuary; 178 (UP), Charlie Hamilton James/National Geographic Image Collection; 178 (LO), Charlie Hamilton James/National Geographic Image Collection; 179 (UP), Charlie Hamilton James/National Geographic Image Collection; 179 (LO), AFRICAN PEOPLE AND WILDLIFE FUND/National Geographic Image Collection; 182 (jaguar), Ana Vasileva/Shutterstock; 182 (leopard), Eric Isselee/Shutterstock; 182 (snow leopard), clarst5/Shutterstock; 183 (tiger), apple2499/Shutterstock; 183 (cheetah), Eric Isselee/Shutterstock; 183 (lion), Eric Isselee/Shutterstock; 183 (cougar), Anan Kaewkhamm/Shutterstock

Published by National Geographic Partners, LLC

Since 1888, the National Geographic Society has funded more than 14,000 research, conservation, education, and storytelling projects around the world. National Geographic Partners distributes a portion of the funds it receives from your purchase to National Geographic Society to support programs including the conservation of animals and their habitats. To learn more, visit natgeo.com/info.

For more information, visit nationalgeographic.com,
call 1-877-873-6846, or write to the following address:

National Geographic Partners, LLC
1145 17th Street N.W.
Washington, DC 20036-4688 U.S.A.

For librarians and teachers: nationalgeographic.com/books/librarians-and-educators

More for kids from National Geographic: natgeokids.com

National Geographic Kids magazine inspires children to explore their world with fun yet educational articles on animals, science, nature, and more. Using fresh storytelling and amazing photography, *Nat Geo Kids* shows kids ages 6 to 14 the fascinating truth about the world—and why they should care. **natgeo.com/subscribe**

For rights or permissions inquiries, please contact National Geographic Books Subsidiary Rights:
bookrights@natgeo.com

Designed by Sanjida Rashid

The publisher would like to thank Ariane Szu-Tu, project editor; Grace Hill Smith, project manager; Lori Epstein, photo director; Vivian Suchman, managing editor; Molly Reid, production editor; Anne LeongSon and Gus Tello, associate designers; and Professor William J. Murphy of Texas A&M University. The authors would like to thank National Geographic photo editor Kathy Moran for guiding Steve through each of his big cat stories, and Veronica Sharon for photo management and editing.

Hardcover ISBN: 978-1-4263-7319-0
Reinforced library binding ISBN: 978-1-4263-7450-0

Printed in South Korea
22/SPSK/1